I0421232

Edible Wild Plants and Useful Herbs

by John Tomikel

ALLEGHENY PRESS
ELGIN, PENNSYLVANIA 16413

TROUT LILY

Dedicated to the science of edible wild foods.

A small notice appeared in a newspaper in 1973 that Euell Gibbons would be a featured speaker at a wild foods gathering at North Bend State Park located near Parkersburg West Virginia. .John Tomikel had published his first book on Edible Wild Plants at that time and he opted to attend the meeting where he met the legendary author. However, as he later stated, he was more enthralled by the woman who had organized the meetings called Nature Wonder Weekend, the personable Edelene Wood who had encyclopedic knowledge of the edible wild. Edelene became the first president of the National Wild Foods Association. In her capacity as president of that organization she invited the foremost wild food writers in America to be guest speaker at the annual Nature Weekend in West Virginia. As John once remarked, she knew more about wild foods than any of them. She became a personal friend of John Tomikel and his family who participated in Nature Wonder Weekend for more than forty-five years. At this writing, Edelene Wood, well into her nineties, is there in West Virginia preparing this year's menu of wild flora and fauna and speaker list for the 2015 Nature Weekend. It is with great pleasure we dedicate this classic reprint to her.

Edelene Wood

This publication is a reprint of the classic work by Dr. John Tomikel. The text was duplicated from the original material and so some pages may not be in exact orientation. We were able to obtain a copy and reproduce it from the original publication.

ISBN   978 1514891216   and   1514891212

original ISBN 0-910042-52-7

Library of Congress Catalog Number   85-52429

If you purchased this book from Amazon or Kindle you can write an opinion or a review of it by going to Amazon Books and clicking on the title. Thank you.

CONTENTS

Blueberries don't all ripen at the same time. Page 45

Figure 2: The late Euell Gibbons, center, and John Tomikel, right, lead a discussion of edible wild plants at a seminar at North Bend State Park, West Virginia.

EUELL GIBBONS REMEMBERED

Ten years ago I sat with Euell Gibbons on a park bench in West Virginia. We were answering questions and having a discussion about edible wild plants with a group of naturalists. Three months later Euell Gibbons was dead.

Probably no one knew more about edible wild plants than Euell Gibbons. His mind was like a sponge continually sopping up vast bits of information about the edible wild and then sharing this knowledge with others.

Euell Gibbons came along at the right time - when the "hippies" were leading the country back to nature and the land. There were many others knowledgeable in the wild plant field but it was Gibbons who became the spokesman. Gibbons appeared on the Tonight Show with Johnny Carson. Carson's jibes and Gibbons' witty retorts catapulted Gibbons into national fame and his name quickly became synonymous with wild food gathering.

After the publication in 1962 of his first book *Stalking The Wild Asparagus*,

Gibbons began to speak to small groups of wild food enthusiasts. One such group was Nature Wonder Weekend, held each September in North Bend State Park in West Virginia. A dynamic woman named Edelene Wood organized the weekend and she became one of Gibbons' main supporters, offering him encouragement, arranging other speaking engagements, and pushing his books. It was partly through her efforts that Gibbons eventually became known enough to be invited on the Tonight Show.

Despite his fame and his increasingly busy schedule Gibbons never forgot Edelene Wood and North Bend State Park. He faithfully returned to the festival every September. One year he and his wife, Freda, flew in from Haiti, another year from the Fiji Islands. Wherever he was in the world he always made it back to West Virginia for the third weekend in September. We who were part of the edible wild world basked in his light.

In 1972 I wrote a small book called *Edible Wild Plants of Pennsylvania and New York*. That year was also the first I heard about Nature Wonder Weekend. I packed my camper and headed for Wild Wonderful West Virginia hoping to learn more about wild foods and to meet the famous Euell Gibbons.

I was not disappointed. I found Gibbons to be a pleasant friendly fellow, generous with his time and willing to chat with anyone standing around. He looked at my name tag and then proceeded to tell me about six short-comings in my book. My expression must have been one of total disbelief, not at my shortcomings, but that he recognized my name and was familiar with my book which had only been out about two months.

After that meeting I attended the wild food festival each year and came to know Euell Gibbons as a person rather than as a personality. Eventually Edelene Wood put me at the end of the programs to sum up the weekend, give praise to those worthy, and to invite everyone back next year. I was also designated as one of the four yearly field trip leaders. This put me in closer contact with Gibbons.

Euell Gibbons started his edible wild career at the insistence of Freda who also drew illustrations for his books. She agreed to tighten the belt and economize if he would take a year off from high school teaching and write a book about his consuming hobby of edible wild plants. The result was *Stalking The Wild Asparagus*.

Soon Gibbons realized that in order to complete the edible wild series, he would have to do a book on edible seashore items since "asparagus" dealt only with land. Thus came *Stalking The Blue Eyed Scallop*, one of his most popular books.

As years went by Gibbons realized the edible wild was almost limitless and he had left so much out of his first two volumes. So he went back to his typewriter and wrote *Stalking The Healthful Herbs*, *Stalking The Good Life*, *Stalking The Faraway Places*, and *The Beachcomber's Handbook*. All of these books were commercial successes and maintained his popularity. By this time Gibbons was the official "guru" of the back-to-nature movement.

In *Stalking The Healthful Herbs* Gibbons emphasized the fact that he and Freda did not live on wild foods. Instead, they "had lunch" with nature or else tried to get one wild item on each day's menu. He referred to the wild food as "ornaments in our cuisine". He also emphasized that he and Freda were "not food faddists in any sense of the term". Eating wild foods was more of a philosophical statement with them.

"If I live to be a hundred," he once said, "I don't think I'll be able to get it all down on paper." Writing was sandwiched between heavy travelling, speaking engagements and commitments to his advertising sponsors. It was a schedule which eventually taxed his strength and contributed to his death at age 64.

Unfortunately with his fame there came a loss of privacy. It became nearly impossible for Gibbons to carry on normal relationships with people in the places he visited. Once, at North Bend he was constantly hounded by the over-enthusiastic president of a wild food foraging club in Chicago. Bob Rogers, Superintendent of North Bend State Park, sized up the awkward situation and told the man to stop it. But the man persisted until Rogers finally told him to get his belongings and leave the park. Such embarassing incidents became more and more a part of Gibbons' life.

Also, unfortunately with fame Gibbons became depicted as a one-dimensional character, a slightly crackpot wild plant eater. This was most unfair as Gibbons was educated, well spoken, and serious minded with expertise in politics, psychology, sociology, psychic phenomena, geology, meteorology, and oceanography. He was an accomplished poet.

"People think I'm very successful," he said to a few of us during a wild coffee break (He had concocted wild coffee from baked and pulverized dandelion roots.), "but I don't feel very successful. There is so much more I want to accomplish, so much more of the world to see, so much to learn."

Once he was sponsored by the U.S. Department of Agriculture on a field trip to Haiti to discuss agriculture problems there with native farmers. He was very impressed with the average Haitian's knowledge of wild plants. According to Gibbons, nine year old Haitians could identify any wild plant he pointed to and could give him a run-down of its attributes and uses.

Euell Gibbons had enjoyed a mere ten years in his place in the sun when he died of a heart attack in 1975. Those who knew him were not surprised; he was constantly under the pressures of fame and the rigors of protecting the investments of his advertisers. During his last years his schedule became impossibly heavy.

In the year prior to his death Euell and Freda were filming life on Fiji and other Pacific Islands. He spoke at great length about the islanders and their life style of living off the land, in this case the shoreline. The film was never released.

Freda Gibbons was a prime motivator in Gibbons' career. She is a fine artist and many of the "stalking" books contain examples of her work. Those who knew her in those "wild" days knew her as a warm, friendly, outgoing individual. She resented being called "Mrs. Euell Gibbons" and preferred to be addressed as Freda Gibbons, a person in her own right.

The main contribution of Euell Gibbons to our society was his leadership in the ecological movements of the 1960's and early 1970's. It is this legacy of environmental concern first publicized by Rachel Carson, Aldo Leopold, and others which still continues to this day. The Environmental Movement has not won the war but it is at last winning battles. We who are a part of that movement will always remember Euell Gibbons as one of our generals.

Sow thistle   Sonchus oleraceus   page 127

I
INTRODUCTION WITH NOTES ON PREPARING
THE PLANTS FOR CONSUMPTION

Bloodroot flowers   see page 151

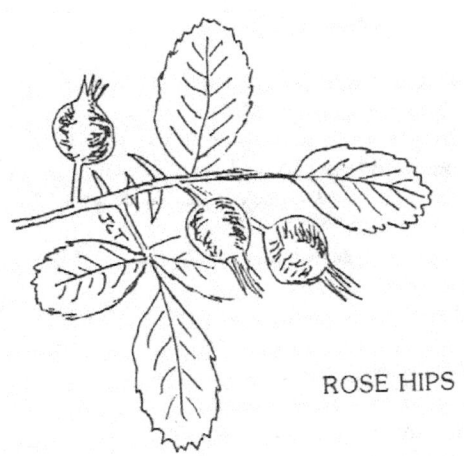

ROSE HIPS

Plants are the bottom rung on the ladder of life and upon which all higher forms in the ecological system are dependent. Humans have utilized all plants in some form or other. Plants have provided humans with food, clothing, housing, bedding, dyes, utensils, esthetics, and animal forage: the list is endless and just the mere mention of some of these easily stresses the point.

This book is concerned with the nutritional aspects of plants and it deals with the more common edible plants found in the United States and Canada. In my first book on edible wild plants I stated that it was "not written as a survival manual" and then proceeded to list most all edible species of the area involved. This work differs in that I do not mention all edible species known to me and I omit species which are edible but not worth the effort of gathering and preparation. Such plants as jack-in-the-pulpit and black locust may have edible parts under proper preparation but these are such fringe plants that it is a disservice to the reader to occupy time with them and these along with many others are omitted. So, what will be found in this volume are those plants which I deem to be most tasty and edible and commonly found.

Purpose of This Book

The idea behind this work is to provide a usable illustrated reference which is inexpensive to the wild plant hobbyist. Gathering and eating wild plants is a hobby. I hate to put it in these terms since there is a hard core of people suspicious of the future and presently training for survival and to them this is no humorous matter.

Two groups of nature enthusiasts that receive smiles from the uninitiated are bird watchers and wild plant gatherers. I happen to fall into both categories and the good natured ribbing that I beget is a small price to pay for the bountiful rewards I receive from being a bit closer to nature than my smirking brethern. When I gave my first book to a friend as a gift he stated "I hope you sell a pile of these, then you won't have to eat this stuff anymore."

To me, eating wild plants is a mystical experience and I have to be careful or I may be carried away emotionally. To many of my wild food friends it is a religious experience of the first caliber and they are obviously over the deep end of some form of reality. They argue over the values of organic versus chemical fertilizer, wild plants versus domesticates, and plants versus meats. I have grown the same species of carrot under organic fertilizer and chemical fertilizer conditions and was unable to detect any difference in the taste. I didn't analyze them for nutrition and so this argument is still open and I wish to be excluded from it.

I state that gathering wild plants is a hobby which could be useful if survival conditions exist. For the average person though, it will remain an inexpensive hobby. It is cheaper than most hobbies since special equipment and clothing are not needed. Unless one forages his own backyard it is not as inexpensive as buying commercial vegetables. I once walked six miles to get a piece of ginger root. Was the time spent worth more than commercial ginger? To me it was but to an economist it would probably not be.

There are several ideas on eating wild plants that have been passed on to me over the years. One is that if a wild plant was worthwhile as a food it would be cultivated in fields and gardens. Of course many of our wild plants are domesticates which have escaped and all domesticated plants are descendents of wild varieties. Many domesticates and wild plants are fringe varieties which please only a few palates. If it were up to me the sweet potato would not be commercially grown since I eat the vegetable only about once a year and then under protest. I will have to agree with those who hold that the plant must not have universal appeal if it is not domesticated. However, the few times a year that the wild plant is eaten makes the search for them worthwhile and the senses are pleased for the moment.

Poisonous Plants

In my youth and in my growing age I have been told that such-and-such a plant was poisonous by various persons. I have strived to eat the plants mentioned in this work in one form or another. Those that I did not eat have been crossreferenced thoroughly or eaten by persons known to me. In this respect questionable plants have been eliminated from the work or designated as questionable. Regarding the poisonous plants, I was shocked and surprised when I read in a reputable text that the wild parsnip was poisonous. My boyhood friends and I spent many afternoons pulling up these plants along the cinder railroad embankments and dining on the roots which we called wild carrot. Only after taking botany in college did I learn that it was known as wild parsnip.

If you were asked to name poisonous plants you would probably list dogbane, poison ivy, or water hemlock. You should be naming such plants as tomato, potato, peach, and a host of plants growing around the home. You see, we only eat certain parts of the plants. It is not different in the wild, in many instances only a limited portion of the plant is edible. This book tries to identify those portions. For the more common wild poisonous plants, refer to Section I of this book. Where portions of edible plants are poisonous then these are mentioned where they are listed in the text.

Use of Scientific Names

One cannot entirely rely on common names for identification of plants. Everyone knows what the dandelion looks like, however, other names may be suspect. There are many varieties of plants which are called pigweed, therefore I have used scientific names for all the plants listed. If one is unfamiliar with the wild plant names then he would be wise to have a flower guide, weed guide, or tree guide in his possession when using this book. These can be referenced to the scientific names. The value of scientific names is that only one plant can have the name and the plant cannot be known by any other scientific name. It must be remembered that two names make up the scientific name, for example, *Taraxacum officinale* is the dandelion. Many other plants use the first name or the last name but only the Dandelion uses the complete name. Different forms of dandelions use different last names which is the specific name, the first name is the generic name and identifies closely related species. Hence, in the oak family we have *Quercus alba* the white oak, *Q. montana* the chestnut oak, and *Q. velutina* the black oak. Notice that once the generic name is used and a sequence follows the generic name may be abbreviated. The specific name is never abbreviated.

Proceed Slowly in Eating

In beginning to eat a new variety of wild plant the diner should proceed slowly, perhaps eating a small portion the first time. Then he should be cognizant of his gastric condition. Some plants may have a laxative effect, others may cause stomach gases to build up, others may simply cause heartburn. People who dined with me on wild plants have been known to complain of those symptoms mentioned when the plant had not affected me. My personal major complaint has dealt with aftertaste in such things as nuts and the bitterness of some roots which usually lose their bitterness after boiling. As a general rule, if one is cautious he may throw away the first water of cooked greens, this would eliminate aftertaste and laxative qualities of some plants for most people.

Methods of Preparation

Basically wild plants are prepared for consumption the same as domestic plants. If it resembles spinach then it can be cooked as you would cook spinach, that is providing the plant is edible. Below is a listing of some basic preparations of plant parts. However, you can use these in any recipe that you can use similar domestic plant parts.

Most recipes for wild plants state that the plant should be boiled, drained, buttered, salted, and peppered. This is so universal a method of preparation that shoe leather is made palatable by this system. Get some variety by trying other recipes.

NOTE: This is a general listing applying only to edible plants. Refer to the specific plant in this text for recommended methods of preparation in case there are any.

roots—eat raw, peel and eat raw, boil, roast, deep fry, pulverize and use as floor for breads, roast some species roots and use as a coffee substitute.

stems—eat raw, peel and eat inner parts raw, cook as you would cook asparagus, unless starving, confine yourself to young tender plants.

leaves—use raw as salad greens, cook as spinach greens, use in making tea, in some cases the first and perhaps second boiling water must be discarded when cooking bitter greens.

flowers—use raw in salads, ferment for wine, pickle pods.

twig buds—eat raw or roasted.

fruit—same uses as apple like fruits or single seeded fruits.

seeds—same uses as oats for grass like seeds and nuts for tree seeds.

II
POISONOUS WILD PLANTS

Psilocybe zapotecorum   a hallucinogenic mushroom

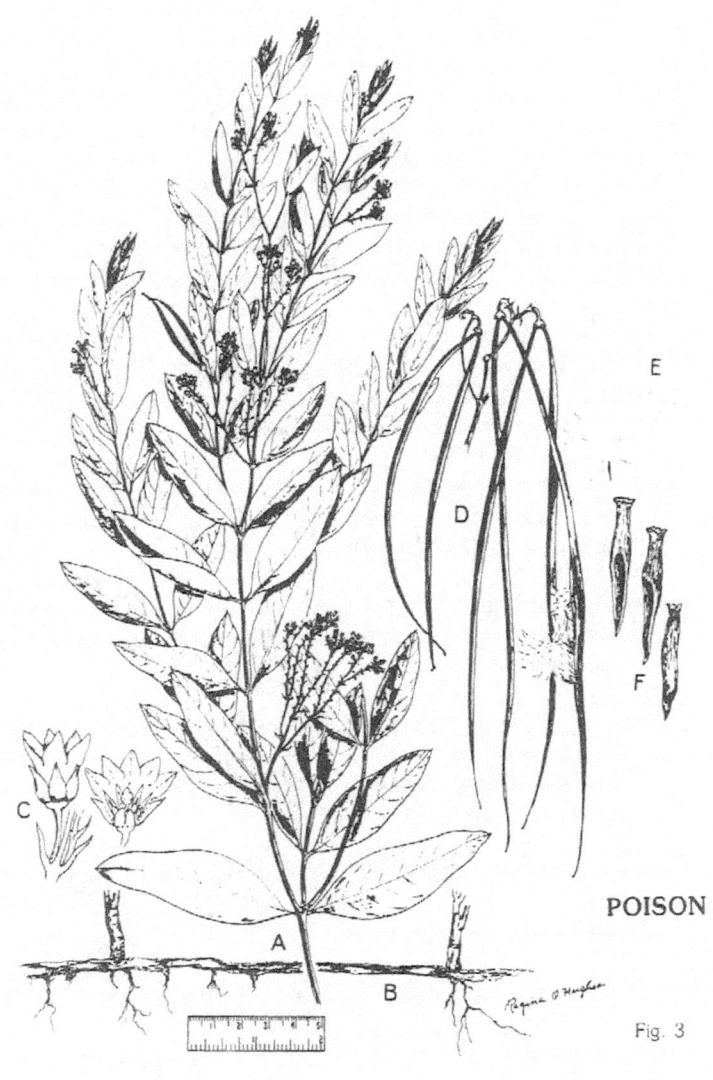

POISON

Fig. 3

DOGBANE *Apocynum cannabinum*   A. habit B. rootstock C. flowers
D. follicles E. seeds

A

B

C

D

Regina O. Hughes

POISON

Fig. 4

JIMSONWEED *Datura stramonium* A. habit of growth B. leaf C. ripe
capsule D. seeds

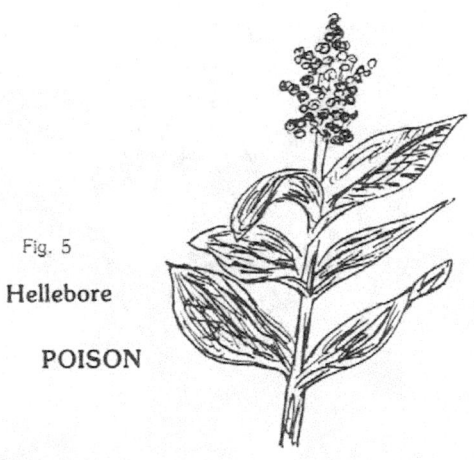

Fig. 5

Hellebore

POISON

DOGBANE   *Apocynum cannabinum*   Figure 3

The dogbane has a round stem which secretes a milky juice. Its leaves are oblong and its stem forking. Its flowers are bell-shaped. This plant can be separated from milkweed since milkweed does not have forking stems. Dogbane is not fatal to healthy humans but eating it could cause much distress.

JIMSON WEED   *Datura stramonium*   Figure 4

This poisonous plant is coarse and loosely branched and grows to a height of four feet in good soil. Its leaves are large and coarsely toothed. The flowers are white or violet and are borne in the forks of the stem. The fruit is egg shaped and resembles a prickly apple which can be cracked into four parts. It is a native of waste lands, vacant lots, and along roadsides. It loves rubbish heaps. It is poisonous.

HELLEBORE   *Veratrum viride*   Figure 5

The Hellebore is one of the first plants to emerge in spring. Its succulent leaves look edible but they are poisonous. It is found along streams and in wet woods and swamps. Flowers of the hellebore are greenish white, hanging in clumps. The toxic substances in hellebore will depress the heartbeat and reduce blood pressure. Since it does have some effect on the body it was used in many folk remedies often with disastrous results. Hellebore is used in modern medicine but in carefully measured doses and for specific diseases. This plant is also known as Indian Poke and Corn Lily.

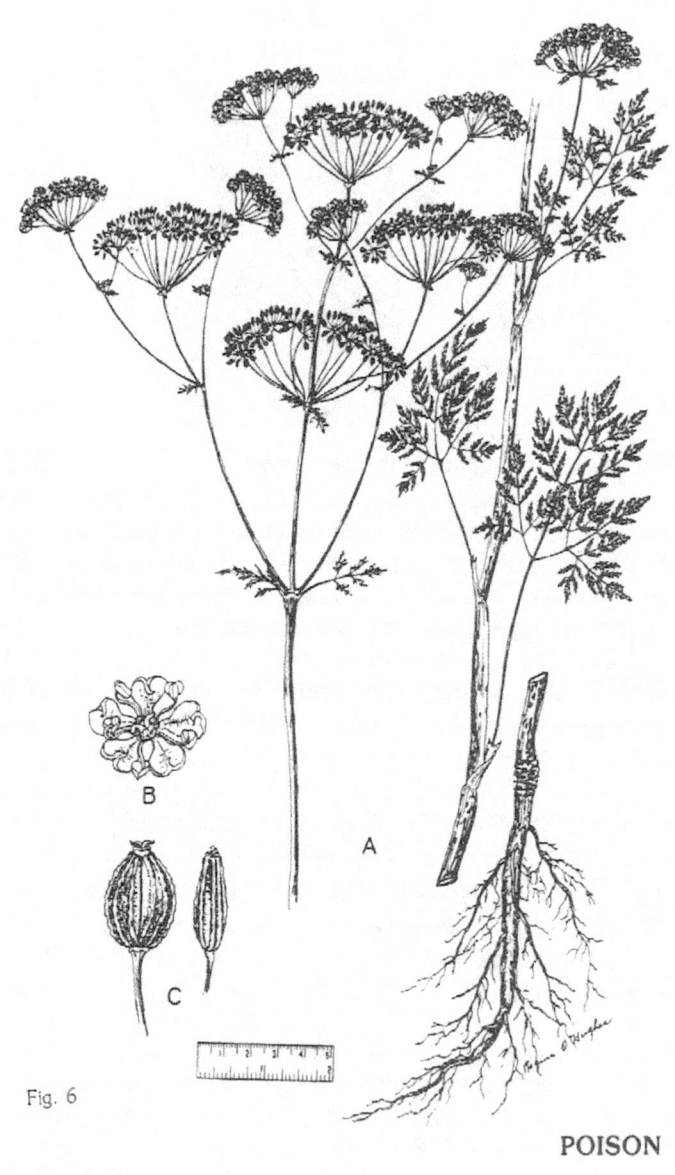

POISON

Fig. 6

POISON HEMLOCK *Conium maculatum* A. habit of growth
B. flower C. seeds

Fig. 7   **POISON**

WATERHEMLOCK *Cicuta maculata* A. habit of growth B. flower
C. seed covering D. seed

Fig. 8

POISON

POISON IVY *Rhus radicans* A. habit of growth B. flower attachment
C. flowers D. drupe E. stones F. aerial roots

POISON
HEMLOCK   *Conium maculatum*   Figure 6

This poisonous plant can be mistaken for Queen Anne's Lace or wild carrot since it inhabits the same environmental niche. The poison hemlock has a long white taproot which is often branched. Its flowers are in large compound bunches. The flowers are white but do not have the concave or bird's nest nature that is characteristic of Queen Anne's Lace. Approach any carrot like plant with a white flower head with caution.

POISON IVY   *Rhus radicans*   Figure 8

It is surprising how many people are allergic to poison ivy and have had its blisters but have not learned to recognize the plant. The plant appears low and in the grass as an upright plant. It may reach as high as three feet on open land. It also twines around trees and posts and then may reach to fifteen feet. The poison ivy leaves are in groups of three with the middle leaf being longer stemmed than the other two. The poison ivy leaf assumes many shapes and it is difficult to depict accurately for the entire mass of forms it takes. The plant develops white waxy berries. The plant should not be eaten or touched.

WATER HEMLOCK *Cicuta maculata*   Figure 7

This poisonous plant appears similar to plants of the carrot family but with much coarser leaves and a thicker and taller stem. The lower leaves are three forked and bear lance shaped or egg shaped toothed leaflets. The stem is smooth, round, and hollow. The white flowers are flat topped and in umbrella like clusters. The root consists of tuber like branches and have a slight parsnip odor. The seeds of the plant are slightly flattened, oblong, and smooth. This plant is extremely dangerous and the eating of it usually ends in death. POISON

Fig. 9

POISON

WHITE SNAKEROOT *Eupatorium rugosum* A. habit of growth
B. branch C. seeds

WHITE
SNAKEROOT

Eupatorium rugosum
E. urticaefolium

Figure 9

This poisonous plant grows three to four feet tall and has opposite, oval leaves which are coarsely toothed. The plant branches upward and has white flower heads which are small but numerous in flat groups. It is found in woodlands and sometimes in meadows. Cows which eat the snakeroot can transmit this poison by way of its milk to humans.

WHITE SNAKEROOT

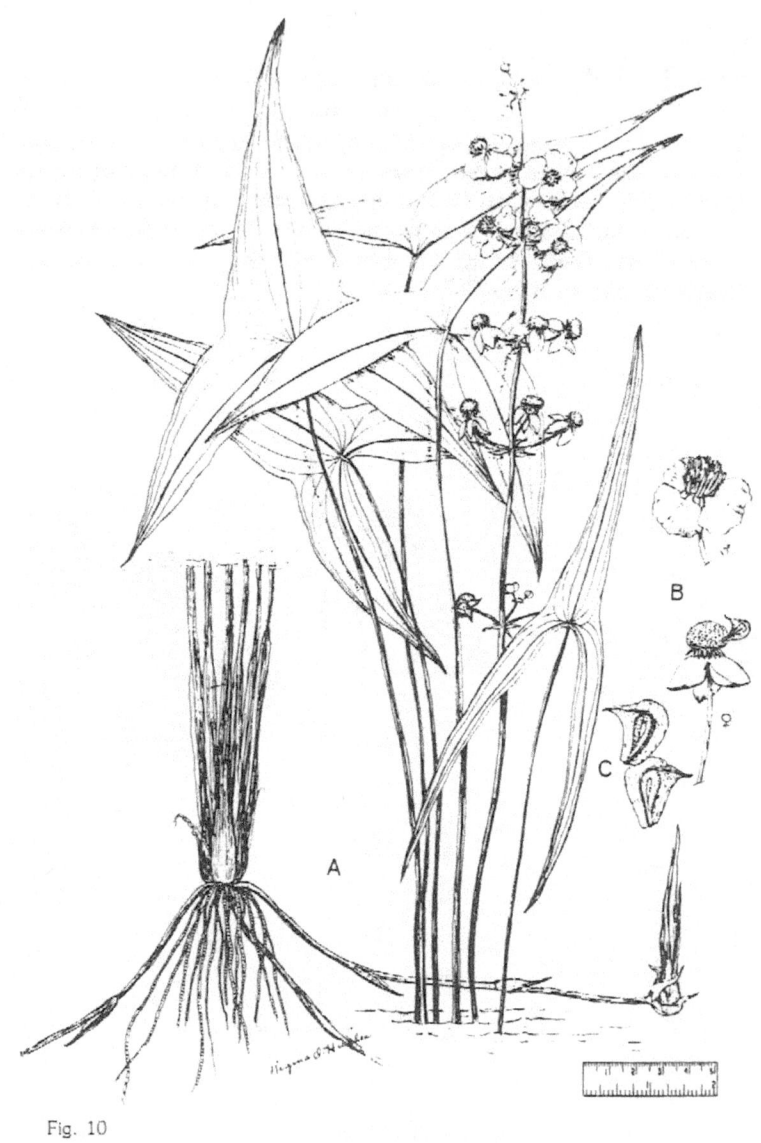

Fig. 10

ARROWHEAD *Sagittaria latifolia* A. habit of growth B. flowers
C. seeds

III
EDIBLE WATER PLANTS

Figure 11: Spatterdock, *Nuphar luteum*

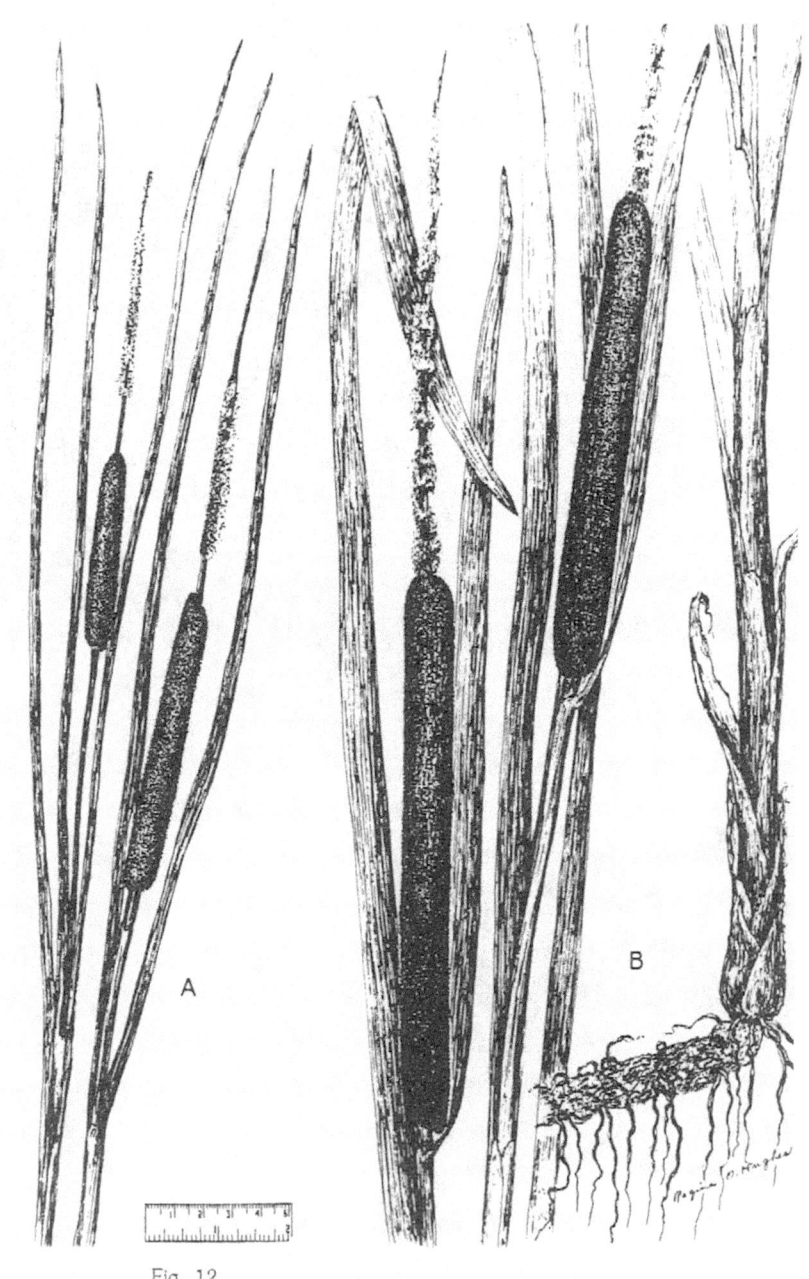

Fig. 12

NARROWLEAF CATTAIL *Typha angustifolia* A. habit of growth
COMMON CATTAIL *Typha latifolia* A. habit of growth

ARROWHEAD   *Sagittaria latifolia*   Figure 10

This aquatic plant grows in shallow water. There is much variation in leaf size and form. The flower is white and about an inch in diameter. The tuberous roots are edible raw but are best boiled and seasoned or roasted on a good hot ash fire. Other names for the plant are arrowleaf, wapatoo, and Tule Potato.

Fig. 13   Calla

Fig. 14   Pickerel Weed

CALLA   *Calla palustris*   Figure 13

The wild calla, also known as Water Arum, is a native of northern bogs and swamps. It is usually found in black muck but can be found in other shallow water areas. It has heart shaped leaves on long stems. The flowers form a mass of greenish white which turn to red berries late in the season. The root may be gathered, pulverized, and used as a bread. The user will have to experiment with this by boiling to suit his own taste.

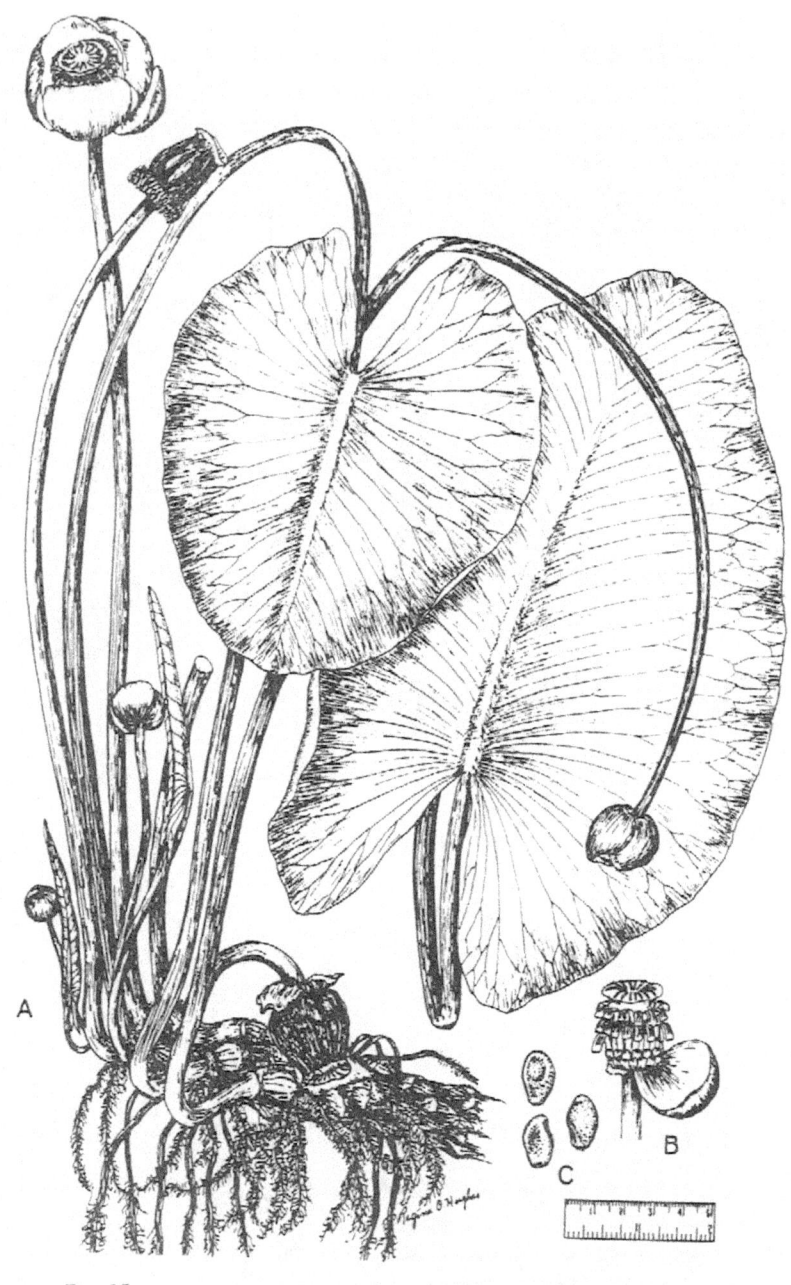

Fig. 15

SPATTERDOCK *Nuphar luteum* A. habit of growth B. petal and
stamen C. seeds

CATTAIL   *Typha latifolia*   Figure 12

This is the tallplant with erect, stiff, reedlike leaves. The root is creeping and branching. The flowers are in dense terminal spikes which finally turn to resemble cotton which shrivels after shedding the pollen. It is a plant of the swamp or wet spot, it is found along the borders of streams and ponds. Almost everything about it is edible. The roots may be peeled and eaten raw or cooked, the greens may be eaten raw or cooked, the flower heads which resemble hot dogs and the pollen they contain may be eaten raw or cooked. The pollen may be used to thicken soups and most parts of the plant may be pickled or used to make jellies. The small cattail, *Typha angustifolia* may be used in a similar manner.

PICKEREL WEED   *Pontederia cordata*   Figure 14

The aquatic pickerel weed is narrower and sturdier looking than the arrowhead which it resembles. Its flowers are violet to purple blue and grow into a spike. The nut like seeds can be used for bread or as a cereal.

SPATTERDOCK   *Nuphar variegatum*   Figure 15

This yellow waterlily has oval or rounded leaves with a heart shaped base. The leaves may be found floating or erect. The flowers are globes of golden thick petals encasing a round knob of seeds. The plant is found on muddy shores or in shallow water. The large rootstocks may be used as a starchy vegetable, the seeds may be used in breads, soups, or popped like corn. The strong flavor of the root may be removed by twice boiling.

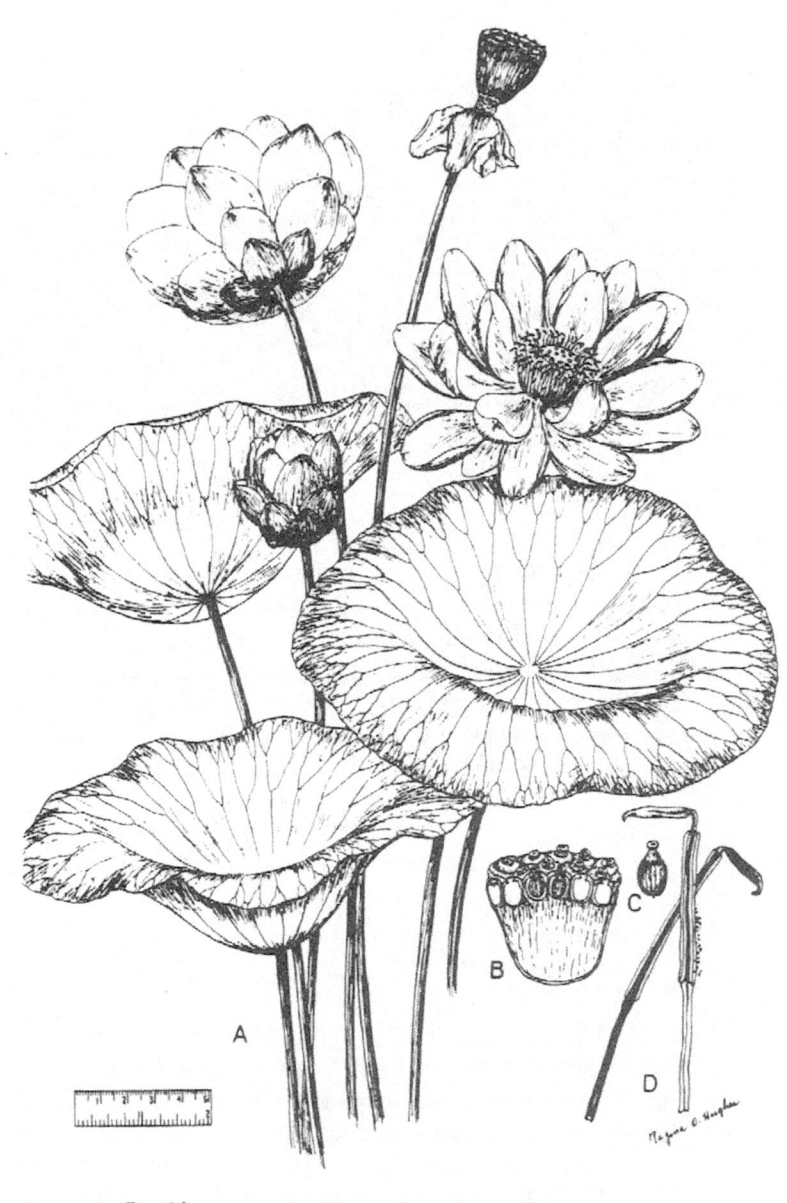

Fig. 16

AMERICAN LOTUS *Nelumbo lutea* A. habit of growth B. pod vertical section C. seed D. stamens

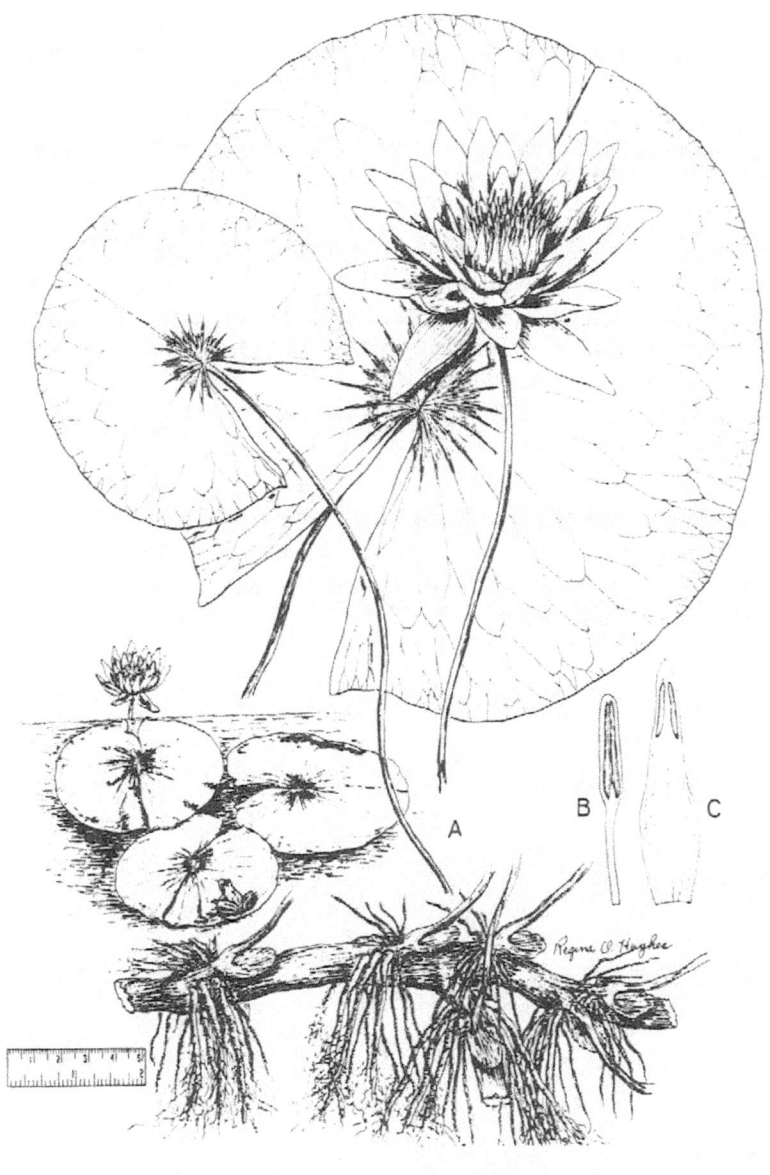

Fig. 17

WATERLILY *Numphaea odorata*   A. habit of growth B. inner stamen
C. outer stamen

WATER LOTUS *Nelumbo lutea* Figure 16

This is the largest of the water lily types. It is also known as American water lotus and water chinquapin. Its leaves can get as large as two feet across and these are often raised above the water surface. The flowers are pale yellow and form a flat topped fruit with large nutlike seeds peering from holes. The tuberous roots are edible and make excellent breads. The new leaves may be used as greens. The large seeds are best used in a half ripe condition. When fully ripe the seeds must be cracked before being roasted or boiled. When dried they can be ground and used in making bread. Do not collect this plant unless there is an abundance.

WHITE
WATER LILY *Nymphaea ampla* Figure 17

This white water lily has many small petals which grow to two inches in length. The edible parts are the seeds and the tuberous roots which bear round or oval shaped masses which are easily broken off for collecting.

IV

EDIBLE SHRUBS AND TREES

APPLES

There are so many different kinds of wild apples that to classify them on the basis of species is an improbable task. Since I was criticized for leaving this out of my first book I mention it in passing here. To make applesauce, take the apples, slice and simmer them in a small amount of water until tender. Press the apples through a coarse sieve or grind or chop them up until the desired texture is reached. Sweeten to taste. Reheat the sauce until it boils and then pack hot into jars; process as you would other canned goods. For immediate eating just reheat until the desired temperature is reached and/or serve cold.

ASH — *Pyrus and Sorbus species*

The mountain ash resembles a cross between a sumach and a walnut tree. It is found in mountainous country or hill regions. The fruit is a large red cluster of berries which can be used for making jelly, dried and used for making bread, or crushed and steeped for making tea. The berries may be eaten raw but are palatable only when mushy ripe.

Fig. 18   Barberry

BARBERRY — *Berberis canadensis*   Figure 18

This prickly plant is found along fence rows, in rocky pastures, and near wood borders. The leaves are about an inch and a half long, and are rounded at the tip and taper toward the base and are sawtoothed. The flowers are pale yellow and droop. The plant is thorny. Its berries are orange red when ripe. Use the berries cooked, in pies, in jellies or eat them raw. The young leaves are also edible. The sap of the wood can be used for a yellow dye.

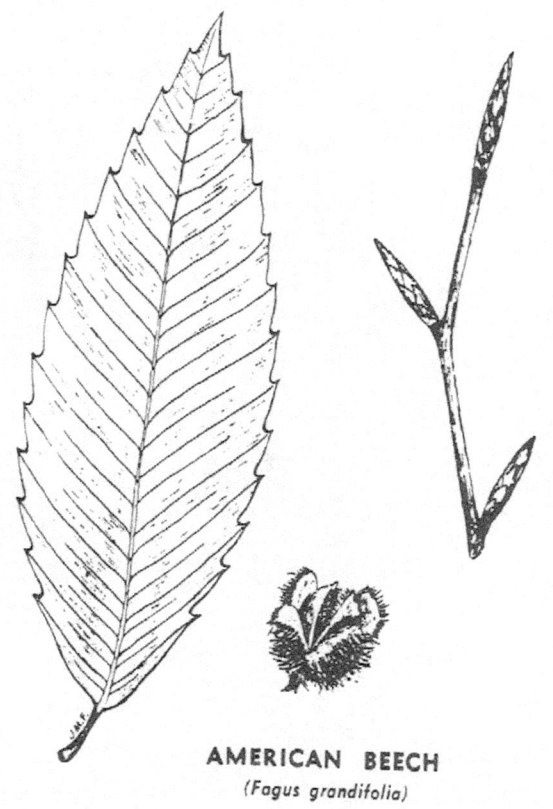

AMERICAN BEECH
(Fagus grandifolia)

Fig. 19

BEECH   *Fagus grandifolia*   Figure 19

The American Beech has long sharp toothed leather leaves, the leaves are yellow green with silky hairs below. The edible buds are red brown and pointed. Beech bark is smooth and never furrowed and the fruit is a brown shiny nut of triangular shape. There are usually two nuts enclosed in a stalked prickly bur which splits when ripe. The beech is found in woodlands and matures to a large tree. The nuts are delicious.

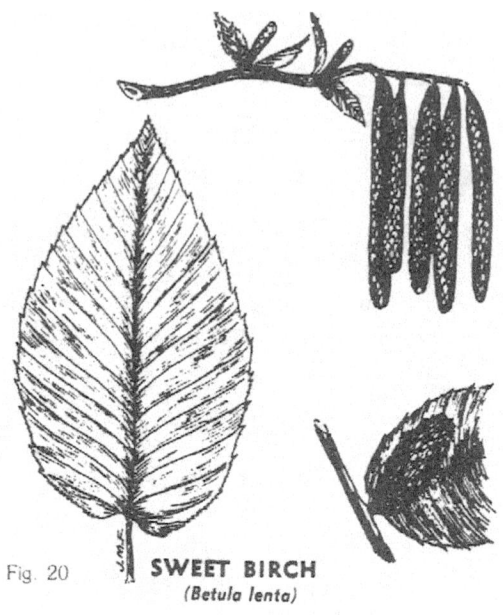

Fig. 20   **SWEET BIRCH**
(Betula lenta)

SWEET BIRCH   *Betula lenta*   Figure 20

The sweet birch is also known as black birch. The inner bark of this tree has the odor of wintergreen. Its catkins are about three inches long. The leaves are heart shaped at the base and pointed at the apex. The sap may be made into various brews such as wine, vinegar, birch beer, and syrup. The young twigs may be used to make tea. The bark from the roots can also be used for tea. The inner bark makes a good flour when dried and pulverized.

WHITE BIRCH   *Betula alba*

The white birch is also known as paper birch. Like the sweet birch its inner bark may be used as a flour, it's excellent when mixed with regular wheat flour. The leaves can be used to make tea, and an interesting wine may be made from the sap.

Making Birch Beer

Add 3-1/2 pints of molasses to 7 quarts of boiling water, mix thoroughly and allow to cool for about three hours. To this add a mixture of about 1/2 pound of crushed black birch bark and sassafras bark or root. Mix these and add a half teaspoon beer yeast or baker's yeast, mix again and add four gallons of water. Allow this to ferment for three to four days if you want an alcoholic beverage and only one day for a mild beer. Keep the three day beer away from children. Once you get the hang of it you can experiment with other wild flavorings. Instead of water, birch sap, which is almost water can be used for a stronger flavor.

BERRIES

Fig. 21   Blackberry   Fig. 22   Flowering Raspberry

BLACKBERRIES   *Rubus various species*   Figure 21

There are many varieties of blackberries, three of which are listed here. Uses of blackberries are many and well known. The mountain blackberry, *Rubus allegheniensis*, grows to seven feet tall. Older stems are reddish and have very piercing thorns.

Leaves are in clusters of fives or threes and are hairy below. The tall blackberry, *Rubus villosus* can grow to nine feet. It usually has three ovate leaves, downy underneath. The dewberry or running blackberry, *Rubus canadensis*, has trailing stems and are found at the ground level in thick thorny mats. The dewberry does not seem as desirable as the higher blackberries. The dewberry is also classified as *Rubus procumbens*.

BLACKBERRY JAM

Take 8 cups of cleaned berries, combine with 5 cups of sugar and cook, while stirring occasionally, until the boiling point has been reached and the sugar dissolved. Then cook until it thickens to a jell, place in jars and seal with lids or wax.

RASPBERRIES   *Rubus various species*   Figure 22

Raspberries are flattened and mature earlier in the summer than blackberries. Their stems are usually greenish white and have small thorns. The flowering raspberry, *Rubus odoratus*, does not have thorns but sticky hairs which are sometimes like bristles. Its fruit is red. The leaves are large and are usually three to five lobed. The red raspberry, *Rubus strigosus*, has numerous bristles and scattered thorns. The black raspberry, *Rubus occidentalis*, reaches eight feet in length. The leaves are usually in groups of three. This is the most common raspberry and the most desired.

Smooth
Black Currant

Fig. 23

BLACK   Figure 23
CURRANT   *Ribes americanum or R. floridum*

The black currant has smooth branches and smooth berries in long drooping clusters. The shrub is three to five feet tall with leaves which are three to five lobed. The flowers which are greenish white are bell shaped and appear in late April or early May. The currant may be eaten directly or made into pies or jellies.

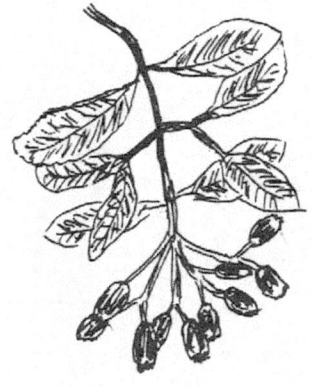

Fig. 25   Blueberry

Fig. 24   Black Haw

BLACK HAW   *Viburnum prunifolium*   Figure 24

The black haw is a large shrub, almost a tree with leaves about
an inch and a half long with a narrow base. The flowers are
in white clusters. The fruit which resembles a small apple like
bud is bluish black when ripe. The condition of the fruit varies
with growing conditions. When a good bush is discovered one
may dine regally from it over a period of many years. Although
the black haws may be cooked they are at their best when eaten
raw.

BLACK
HUCKLEBERRY   *Gaylussacia resinosa*

The black huckleberry or whortleberry grows to about three
feet high and resembles blueberries. It is classed in a different
genus due to its different characteristics of flower and fruit
arrangements. Leaves of the black huckleberry are oval to oblong. Flowers are reddish. The fruit is shiny black and each
contains ten tiny seeds which makes this less desirable than
the blueberries. However, the huckleberry is worth searching
out.

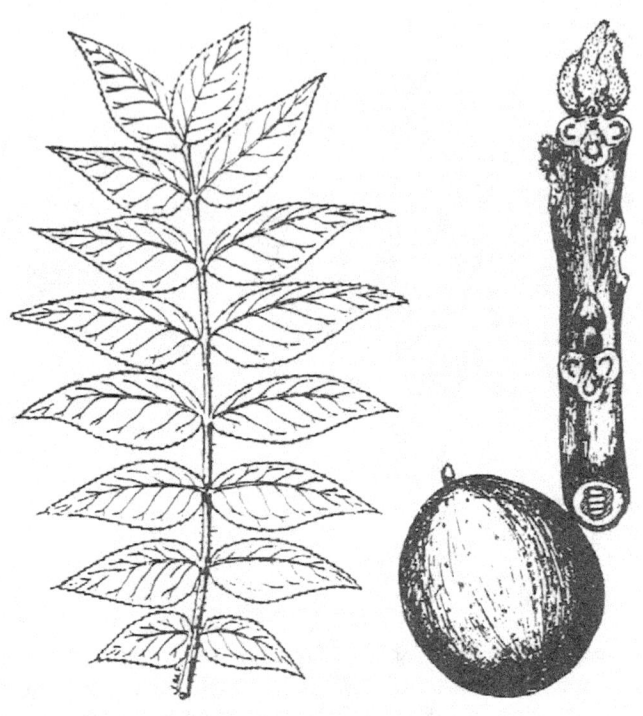

EASTERN BLACK WALNUT
(Juglans nigra)

Fig. 26

BLACK WALNUT   *Juglans nigra*   Figure 26

The valuable wood of the black walnut seems to be spelling its demise. The tree is easily recognized and is presently found along roadsides and fence rows. The nut is hard to crack and is taken from its shell with difficulty. The husk juice which stains ones hands and clothing can be used for dyeing. The kernel is excellent in cookies.

BLUEBERRY　　　　*Vaccinium species*　　　　Figure 25

The blueberry is familiar to every pie lover. There are about a dozen species of blueberries. They are all edible and confusion with other berry types is most difficult. The high bush blueberry grows to fifteen feet. It is also known as swamp blueberry, *Vaccinium corymbosum.* The berries are almost black. The low bush blueberry, *V. pennsylvanicum* grows to a height of about two feet. The late low blueberry, *V. vacillans* grows to a height of three feet and to my experience is the most common of those mentioned. It is more blue than the others and sweeter. However the berries are smaller in size.

HAWTHORN: Crataegus species

WILD
RED CHERRY　　　*Prunus pennsylvanica*

The wild red cherry is also known as fire cherry. It has fruits borne in loose tufts along the small branches. It is very sour and has a thin pulp. It is not worth seeking but it is edible. It is great in jellies.

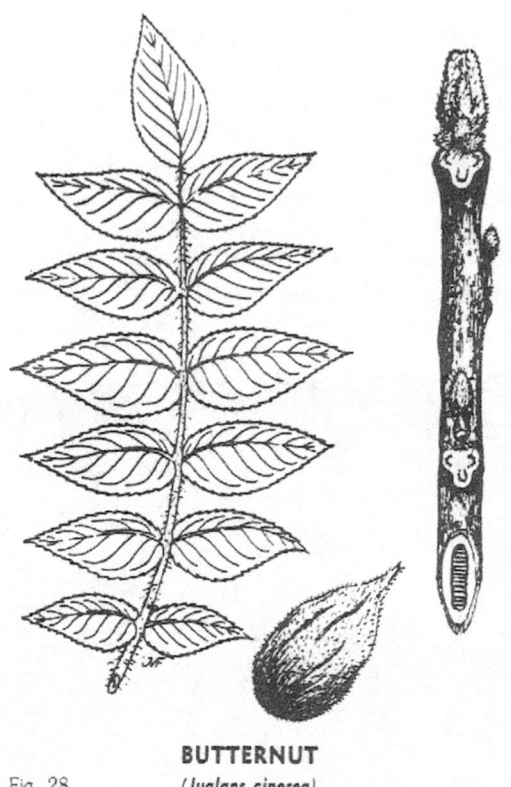

BUTTERNUT

(Juglans cinerea)

Fig. 28

BUTTERNUT *Juglans cinerea* Figure 28

The butternut seems to be rarer than the black walnut and as the years go by seems to be in existence only by accident. It is difficult to find the trees in deep woods and it seems to be the most abundant in back yards. At one time the butternut was a staple of the early Indian diet. The long nut has a sweet oily flavor much milder than the walnut. The deeply furrowed nut is covered by a thin husk. There is no need to dwell on this delicacy but it is mentioned here to remind the reader that it does exist.

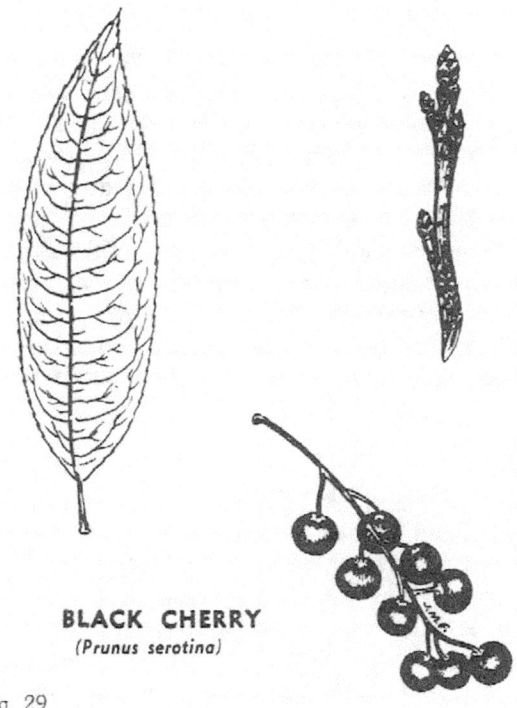

BLACK CHERRY
(Prunus serotina)

Fig. 29

WILD
BLACK CHERRY   *Prunus serotina*   Figure 29

The leaves of the black wild cherry are narrow with a tapering tip, they are shiny above and dull below. The twigs and leaves are bitter when chewed. The black cherry is a large tree. Its flowers are white and hang in clusters. The black to purple fruit is edible and a favorite among winemakers. This tree is much in demand for lumber.

CHOKE CHERRY   *Prunus virginiana*

The choke cherry is similar to the wild black cherry and it takes a concerned individual to tell them apart. The choke cherry is more of a shrub than a tree. The fruit is redder than black. The choke cherry leaves are more oval shaped than the wild black cherry. All three cherries listed have an astringent quality to them.

CRAB
APPLE   *Pyrus angustifolia and P. coronaria*

The crab apples are greenish yellow and very sour. They are best used in preserves and pickled with other fruits. Two types occur in overgrown fields and on the edges of woods. The narrow leaved Crab Apple, *Pyrus angustifolia,* grows to a height of about twenty feet. Its leaves are narrow and glassy and its twigs usually have large thorns. It produces pinkish blossoms in the spring. The American Crab Apple, *Pyrus coronaria,* gets a little larger and it too contains thorns. Its leaves are sharply toothed and often lobed. Its blossoms are rose colored and sweetly scented. These are the fruits which can be put on sticks and whipped across the countryside.

CRANBERRY   Figure 30

The high bush cranberry, Viburnum opulus, has gray brown bark and three lobed leaves which resemble a maple tree. It gets a flat topped cluster of large red berries in late summer. The berries are hard but soften after the first frost. The taste is strongly acid and the berries are best used in jellies or other cooked recipes. Each berry contains a large flat seed. It is from this tree that the Snowball tree of lawn and garden was developed.

Fig. 30   High Bush Cranberry   Fig. 31   Elderberry

48

The low cranberry, Vaccinium macrocarpon, has slender creeping vines growing to two feet in length. Its leaves are evergreen and its flower is pinkish. The fruit is green and turns red in early fall. The berries are best stewed with sugar. They are not palatable in the raw state.

ELDERBERRY   *Sambucus canadensis*   Figure 31

The elderberry can grow to a height of twelve feet in our area. It has pithy upright stems which are excellent for making choke cherry shooters and whistles. Young stems have green bark which eventually turns gray brown. The flower clusters are flat and pie shaped. The berries are purple when ripe and are excellent raw or in pies and jams. The flowers as well as the fruit can be used to make wine. The flower buds are edible and are good pickled.

ELDERBERRY JELLY

For a small batch take 2 quarts of mostly ripe elderberries, stem and wash thoroughly, then place them in a kettle along with 3 cups of water, bring to a boil. Once boiling, reduce the heat and cook for forty minutes with occasional stirring. Strain the resulting juice through a cloth with as little shaking as possible, discard the berries. Add one and a half cups of fine sugar to each cup of juice and bring to a boil over high heat. Once the sugar has dissolved pour into clean glasses and seal with melted jelly wax or paraffin. Don't cook much further than enough to dissolve the sugar.

Figure 32: Gooseberry, *Ribes cynosbati*

GOOSEBERRY *Ribes cynosbati* Figure 32

It is a joy to discover wild gooseberry plants since they seem
to be getting rarer. It is a low shrub with long drooping branches.
The leaves are lobed and are usually in clusters of threes or
fours with a thorn near the base of each cluster. In the spring
the flowers are in groups of three, greenish white in color. The
berries are brown red or brown purple when ripe. They are covered with thorny growths but may occasionally be found smooth.
Watch out for the berry spikes when eating.

Figure 33: Wild grape, *Vitis*

GRAPE *Vitis species* Figure 33

In my youth there was always a rumor that wild grapes were not edible. To my present knowledge they are all edible but sometimes not desirable. They are excellent for wine, in preserves, in jellies, and dried like raisens. The summer grape, *Vitis aestivalis* has lobed leaves with short broad lobes that are rusty woolly underneath. The grapes are small and bluish black. The winter grape, *V. cordifolia* and *V. bicolor*, has leaves which are bluish underneath. The fox grape, *V. labrusca*, has leaves which are opposite tendrils or blossom clusters. It too has rusty wool underneath its leaves. The grapes are large and brownish purple in color. The muscadine, *V. rotundifolia*, is recognized by its unbranched tendrils. Its leaves are small with large blunt teeth. The grapes are in small clusters but each grape is large with thick tough skins. Wild grapes like domestic grapes have good and bad years.

WILD GRAPE WINE

Gather a sizable amount of ripe wild grapes. Wash and pick these clean. Put them into a crock or plastic garbage pail and crush the fruit thoroughly. Add about half as much water as you have fruit juice. Have one teaspoon of wine yeast for each five gallons of batch. You can use ordinary bread yeast for this purpose but a cloudy wine will result. Mix the yeast in a small amount of warm water to get a soupy mess, leave this stand for about a half hour until it becomes frothy and then add this yeast smear to your batch. Wait about four hours and then add about two pounds of sugar for each batch gallon for a dry wine and four pounds of sugar for each batch gallon if you wish a sweet wine. Let this ferment somewhere at a temperature of about 70° F. or room temperature. Cover the batch with a clean cloth. Stir this twice each day until the day the bubbles on top of the wine disappears. When this happens (no longer than the fourth day) transfer the wine into another container by siphoning off the liquid and leaving behind the dregs. You can put it into gallon jugs at this stage. Don't siphon too close to the bottom. It's a shame to waste the bottom wine but this prevents unsightly things from floating around in your finished wine. Fill your jugs to the top leaving just enough room for a cork. Drill a hole in the cork, or purchase one predrilled, and fit it tightly in place, fit it with a piece of plastic tube. Place the other end of the tube in a jar of water, bubbles should appear in the water, if they don't then seal your cork with wax. Bubbles indicate that the fermentation process is still working. Make sure the out end of the hose is in water at all times. You can eliminate the water jar by making a gooseneck in the hose and filling the gooseneck trap with water. When the bubbling stops, the wine is ready. Siphon out the wine and pack into your bottles. Corks are the best stopper. Disturb the batch as little as possible while siphoning. Place the wine in a dark cool place. Wait about a month before trying. The longer you keep the wine the better the quality. Your first batch should be consumed within the first year to see if you did it right. This same recipe can be used for blackberries, choke cherries, elderberries, etc.

GREENBRIER   *Smilax rotundifolia*   Figure 34

The greenbrier is a trailing vine hanging over limbs in the woods. It makes traveling through the woods difficult for it seems to string itself over trails. It develops a cluster of blue black berries in the fall. The roots may be ground into a meal or used in soups. The new growth may be snapped off and eaten raw or cooked.

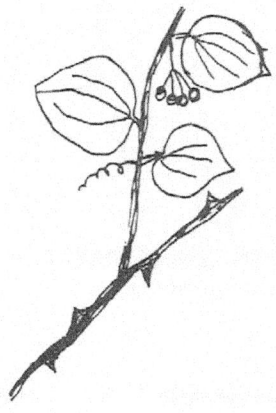
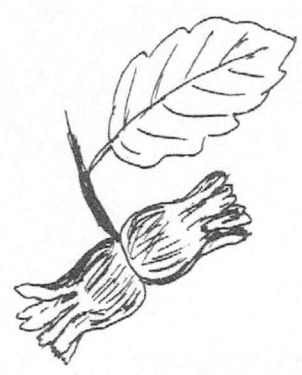

Fig. 34   Greenbrier   Fig. 35   Hazelnut

HAZELNUT   *Corylus americana, C. rostrata*   Figure 35

The hazelnut bush appears as a clump of twigs, branches, and leaves in a hump up to six feet high. Young shoots are covered with thin hairs. The leaves are rounded at the base, sawtoothed and sharp pointed. The blooms hang down in catkins. The plant is more common than most people suspect. The beaked hazelnut, *Corylus rostrata*, is a close relative. It is less hairy and grows in smaller clumps. The husk covering the nut is elongated at the tip, hence its name. When ripe, hazelnuts are sometimes thrown clear of the husk and can be collected at the base of the bush. They are good eating raw or in candies.

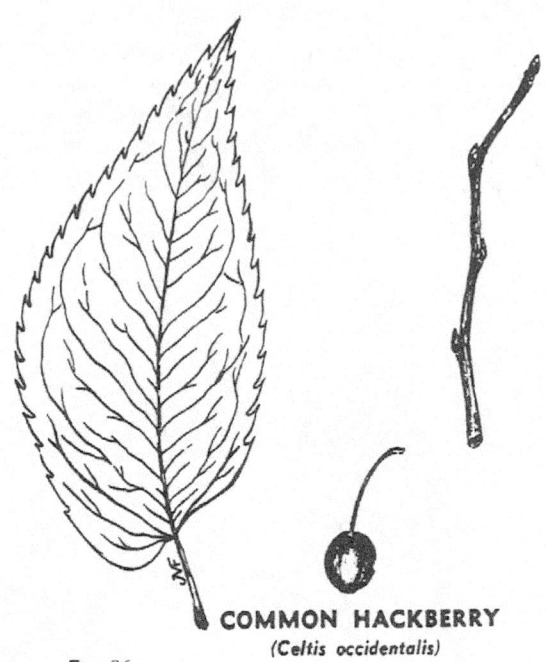

COMMON HACKBERRY
(Celtis occidentalis)

Fig. 36

HACKBERRY   *Celtis occidentalis*   Figure 36

The hackberry is found on hillsides of new woods. The leaves resemble the elm, pointed and saw toothed. The bark is rough and looks like hard cork. The flowers are small and greenish and are found where leaf stems join the twig. The fruit is brown to purple in color and contains a large seed. Some fruits are pulpy and some are mostly seed. Both extremes are pleasant to eat raw.

HAWTHORN   *Crataegus species*

The hawthorns are small trees with lobed leaves and sharp thorns upon the twigs and limbs. They bear white flowers in the spring which occur in clusters as the ripened fruit does in the fall. The ripe fruit contains hard small seeds and are from red to yellow in color. They resemble little apples. These can be eaten raw or used in making jellies and jams.

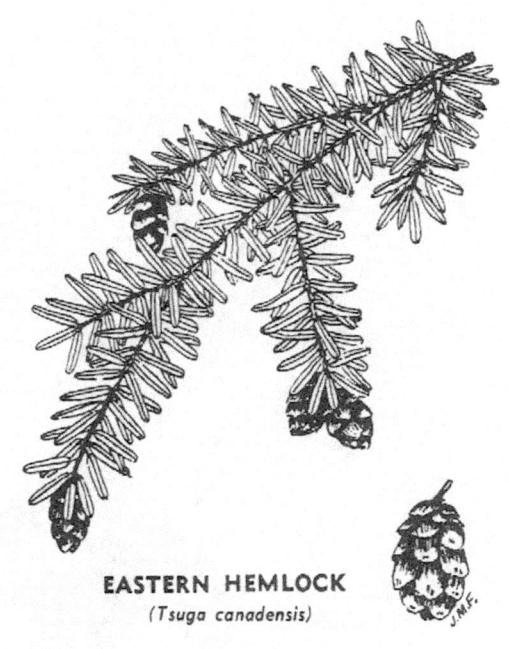

EASTERN HEMLOCK
(Tsuga canadensis)

Fig. 37

HEMLOCK *Tsuga canadensis* Figure 37

The hemlock or eastern hemlock is a small needled evergreen with needles occurring singly and appearing spirally arranged on the twigs. The needles are dark green above and light green below. The seed bearing cones are less than an inch long, egg shaped, and remain attached all winter. It is a tree of the woodland. Its inner bark can be eaten raw or cooked. The needles may be used to make a tea. Do not consume parts of small plants since this may be confused with the American Yew which is inedible except for its berry. See also Yew.

**SHAGBARK
HICKORY**
(Carya ovata)

Fig. 38

HICKORY *Carya species* Figure 38

The hickory is a well known tree with a nut which varies in size and taste according to species and growing conditions. While burning, the wood has a pleasant odor. The husk covering the nut splits into four sections yielding a clean nut. The kernel is small and tasty in the shagbark which gets its name from the loose shaggy appearance of its bark, sometimes it is also referred to as shellbark hickory. Hickory leaves are usually in groups of five. The nut of the shagbark hickory, *C. ovata*, the shellbark hickory, *C. laciniosa,* and the mockernut hickory, *C. tomentosa* are sweet or acceptably sweet. The nut of the pignut hickory, *C. glabra* and the bitternut hickory, *C. cordiformis,* are very bitter with a strong aftertaste.

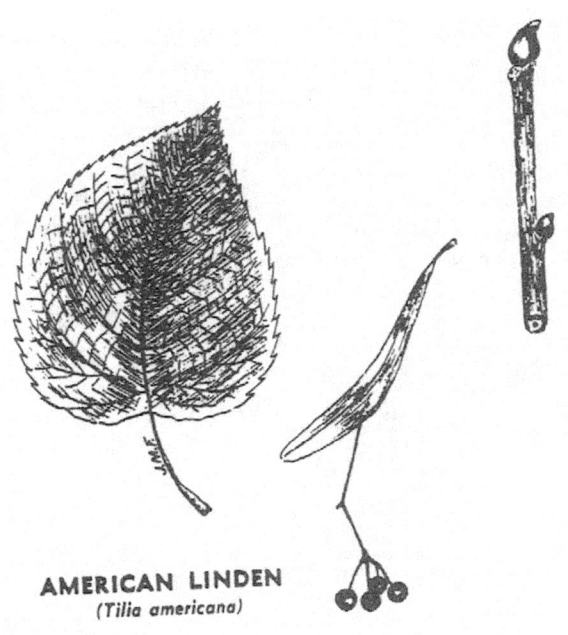

AMERICAN LINDEN
(Tilia americana)

Fig. 39

LINDEN *Tilia americana* Figure 39

The leaves of the linden are heart shaped, shiny dark green on top and smooth duller green below. The margins of the leaves are sharply toothed. Fruit is borne in groups on a long stem and are about the size of a pea. The fruit is attached to a blade or bract. It is a tree of the woodland and is also common along fence rows. The sap of the tree contains a high sugar content and it can be used to make candy. The fruit can be eaten raw in moderation and the flowers can be used to make tea. The buds can also be eaten. The linden is also known as basswood.

LABRADOR TEA   *Ledum groenlandicum*   Figure 40

This plant which is also known as bog tea is a low growing evergreen which reaches a height of about three feet. Its leaves which alternate are one to three inches long and have rolled outer margins. The leaves are wooly brown underneath. They are fragrant when crushed. The plant is a native of the cool north and the highlands of the middle states. To make tea, dry the leaves, steep in water, add sugar and lemon if you wish the flavor complimented.

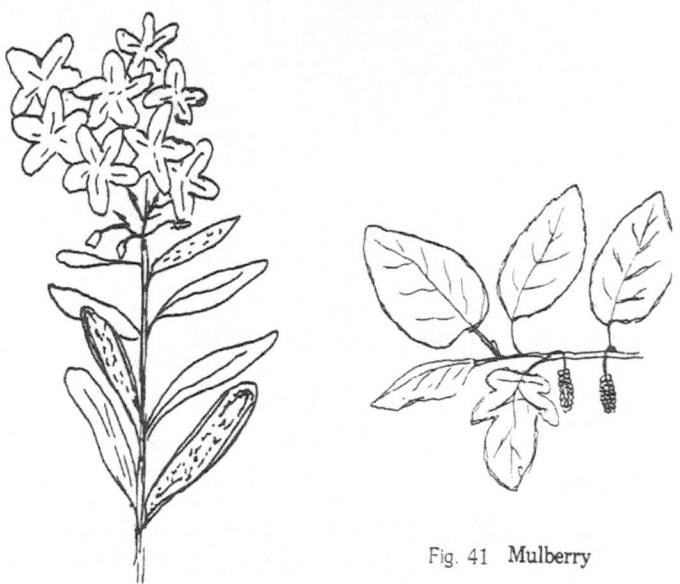

Fig. 41   Mulberry

Fig. 40   Labrador Tea

MULBERRY   *Morus rubra*   Figure 41

This is the berry tree which grows to a height of forty to fifty feet. The leaves are coarse toothed and may be lobed or without lobes. The bark is gray to red brown. The flowers are green and are in spikes or catkins. The edible berry resembles a black-berry, some reaching an inch in length. When edible the berry is red changing to purple. It is sweetest when purple and may be used in pies, jellies, or eaten raw. The white mulberry, Morus alba, is similar to the red in tree habit and growth. Its berries are plumper but have little flavor.

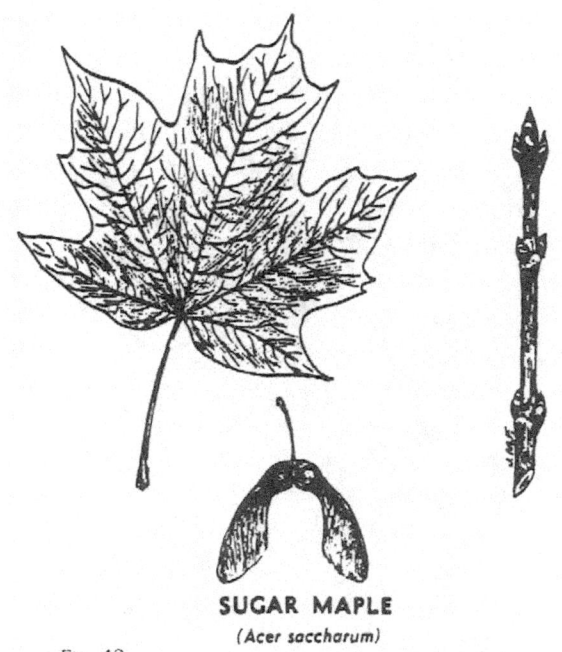

SUGAR MAPLE
(Acer saccharum)

Fig. 42

MAPLE *Acer species* Figure 42

There are many varieties of maple and all of them may be used for making maple syrup, candy, and sugar. The most desirable maple for this purpose is the sugar maple, *A. saccharum*, which has a five lobed leaf with few margin teeth; second in line is probably the silver maple, *A. saccharinum*, which has a five lobed leaf also but with very deep spaces between the lobes. Another common tree is the red maple, *A. rubrum* which has three lobes. The Norway maple, *A. platanoides*, has five lobed leaves but oozes a milky sap when the leaf stem is broken. The Norway maple is the most used for street and commercial tree planting.

WHITE OAK
(Quercus alba)

Fig. 43

OAK   *Quercus species*   Figure 43

The acorns of the oak trees are edible, the white oak, *Quercus alba,* is preferred, the chestnut oak, *Q. montana,* is not bad, and the rest are not too acceptable. The scarlet oak, *Q. coccinea,* has bitter acorns and a second boiling is in order before they are palatable. Acorns may be boiled or roasted, they can be ground into meal for bread making. I am under the impression that the rounded leaved oaks produce palatable acorns and the pointed leaved oaks do not, I may be in error there but check for yourself.

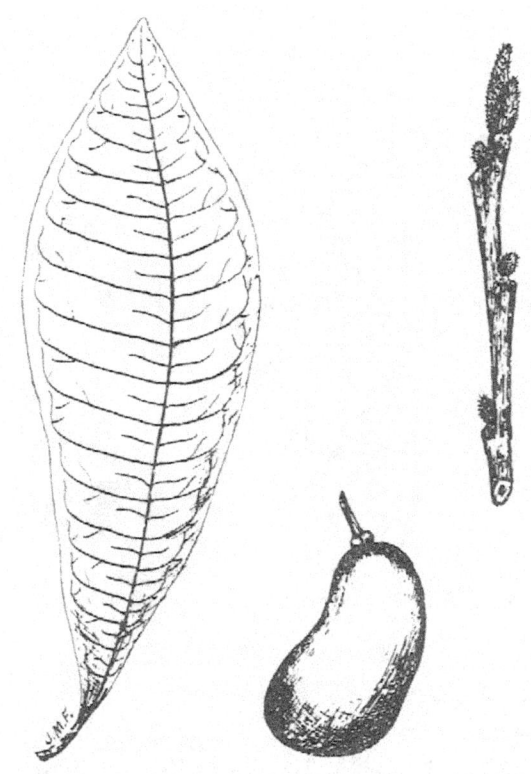

COMMON PAWPAW
(Asimina triloba)

Fig. 44

PAWPAW   *Asimina triloba*   Figure 44

The leaves of this tree are simple and drooping, they are dark green above and light green below. The fruit which is edible appears as a short stubby banana. It contains numerous brown shiny seeds imbedded in a fragrant outer pulp. The flower which generates the fruit is brownish green and appears before the leaves are out. The fruit is edible raw or cooked. If fallen green fruit is found, it may be kept to ripen.

PEAR   *Pyrus communis*

The wild pear is a variety sprung from the cultivated pear which has escaped to the woods. The wild pear fruit is more round than the tame and its branches are usually thorny. The wild pear is ripe in early September. The quality of the fruit apparently varies with growing conditions.

Fig. 45

COMMON PERSIMMON
(Diospyros virginiana)

PERSIMMON   *Diospyros virginiana*   Figure 45

The persimmon is a thin tree with dark deeply furrowed bark.
The flowers are yellow white. The ripe fruit is orange and contains flat seeds. When green the fruit will pucker your mouth
but when ripe it has an interesting sweet flavor. The later in
the season it is picked the more desirable it is.

PINE   *Pinus species*

The inner bark of pine trees can be used as an emergency food,
especially that of the white pine. The seeds of pines are also
edible and can be eaten raw or roasted.

PLUM   *Prunus species*

Wild plums are edible and really more abundant than is suspect-
ed by most people. The chicasaw plum, *Prunus angustifolia* is
red and the Allegheny Sloe plum, *P. alleghaniensis* is deep purple. The wild plum of the east, *P. americana*, is yellow but in
some years produces reddish fruit. These of course can be used
in jams, jellies, and pies or eaten raw.

Fig. 46

MULTIFLORA ROSE *Rosa multiflora* A. habit of growth B. leaf base
C. bud D. bud growth E. fruits F. achenes (pits)

ROSE *Rosa species* Figure 46

Roses are easily recognized and are found in open fields and
on the borders of woods. Rose fruits which resemble little apples
are edible and may be used in many ways, raw or cooked. The
pink rose petals may be used to make an interesting tea.

COMMON SASSAFRAS
(Sassafras albidum)

Fig. 47

SASSAFRAS *Sassafras albidum* Figure 47

The greenish bark, the lobed leaves, and the pleasant smell of the crushed twigs make this tree easily recognized. The leaves may be single, two lobed, or three lobed. They are dark green above and light green below. The tree is found in new woodlands. Its leaves, flowers, stems, twigs, and roots may be used in making tea and flavoring soups. The root is said to be the best for these purposes.

SPRUCE *Picea species*

The young shoots of the spruce tree may be used to make beer and the young needles may be eaten raw if one is hard pressed. The spruces are characterized by their sharp pointed needles. The Norway spruce, *Picea abies,* has the longest needles and its twigs are yellow brown. The red spruce, *P. rubens,* has shorter needles and orange brown twig bark with fine hairs. The black spruce, *P. mariana,* is a smaller tree than the other two but quite common.

Fig. 48   Serviceberry

Fig. 49   Spicebush

SERVICEBERRY   *Amelanchier species*   Figure 48

This juneberry is a shrub that can grow into a large tree if left alone. It develops a white flower which becomes a purple red black berry containing ten seeds. This plant, also known as shadbush, is found in open woods as well as in hedge rows. The berries ripen in late May in the south and ripening progresses northward to Canada when August is the ripening month there. For identification purposes the leaves are somewhat round with sharp toothing, the bark is smooth and grayish. The fruit may be eaten raw or cooked into sauces or made into pies. The berries can also be dried and recovered by simmering in a covered dish.

SPICEBUSH   *Lindera or Benzoic aestivale*   Figure 49

This shrub often springs up on long shoots but bush and tree like growth are also common. The flowers appear in the spring as yellow clusters which change to red berries in the fall. Its leaves are long and similar to choke cherry. It is found in most woodlands and is easy to pass by. Its edible red fruit consists of thin pulp over a large seed. The fruit which has the texture of allspice can be used as a spice in cooking or just chewed as one meanders through the woods. The new bark may also be chewed in the manner one would chew sassafras. A tea may be made by brewing berries, leaves, and twigs.

Fig. 50

SMOOTH SUMAC *Rhus glabra* A. habit of growth B. flowers C. fruit
  D. seeds

SUMAC

Rhus species

Figure 50

This shrub has coarse soft branches and feather like leaves with numerous pointed leaflets. It bears a terminal cluster of red berry like fruits. The flowering blossoms are small and yellow green. The red yellow fruit of the sumac or sumach is edible and is used to make an excellent tea. For lemonade, pour boiling water over the crushed berries, steep to suitable color, add sugar, cool. The poison sumac resembles the others but has white berries and since only the berries are used there should be no mistakes made here.

WHITE CEDAR   *Thuja occidentalis*

The white cedar or American arbor vitae has the odor of cedar oil when cut. Its twigs and new growth may be used to make tea. Hill people have told me that this tea is good for rheumatism but I don't believe it.

WHITE POPLAR   *Populus alba*

The inner bark of the white poplar can be dried and ground into flour for making bread. The inner bark can also be cut into strips and eaten raw or cooked. It makes a nice soup.

WITCH HAZEL   *Hamamelis virginiana*

The witch hazel can be found in most woodlands if a diligent search is conducted. Its leaves resemble a small chestnut oak and its fruit is a seed shot from a double husk. The leaves may be boiled to form a strong tea and the seeds may be eaten but they are oily.

YEW   *Taxus canadensis*   Figure 51

The American Yew is a well known ornamental shrub but it can be found in the woods and on the borders of fields. The waxy red berry is sweet and desirable, however the yew does not produce many of these. The seed is reputed to be harmful but there seems to be no evidence for this. The American Yew is a small evergreen shrub resembling the hemlock tree but the yew has larger needles or leaves. The fruit is a fleshy cup and is best eaten right from the bush. Do not eat the bark or needles, spit out the seed.

Fig. 51 Yew

Figure 52: Purslane, *Portulaca oleracea*

V
EDIBLE LOW PLANTS

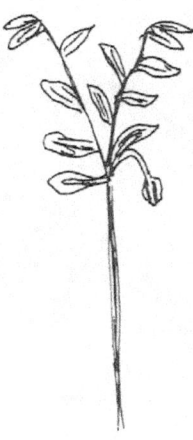

Fig. 53   Bellwort

BELLWORT   *Uvularia sessilifolia*   Figure 53

The bellwort has solitary or paired pale yellow flowers. Its leaves are grayish beneath and rough on the margins. The plant is found in the open woods. The young shoots may be used as cooked greens.

BEAN   *Phaseolus acutifolius*

The wild bean is unknown to most people. It grows on a vine which climbs over bushes or trails along the ground. It resembles the string bean with its three large oval leaves. Its flowers are purple and these eventually turn into short pods about two inches long.

Fig. 54

BLACK MEDIC *Medicago lupulina* A. habit of growth B. flower raceme C. fruiting raceme D. flower E. legume F. seeds

BLACK MEDIC   *Medicago lupulina*   Figure 54

Although this plant resembles clover it is a member of the pea family. Its clover like blossoms are yellow and they produce a small black coiled seed structure. It is found around meadows and along roadsides. The seeds are edible and have a nice flavor when made into paste and spread on crackers.

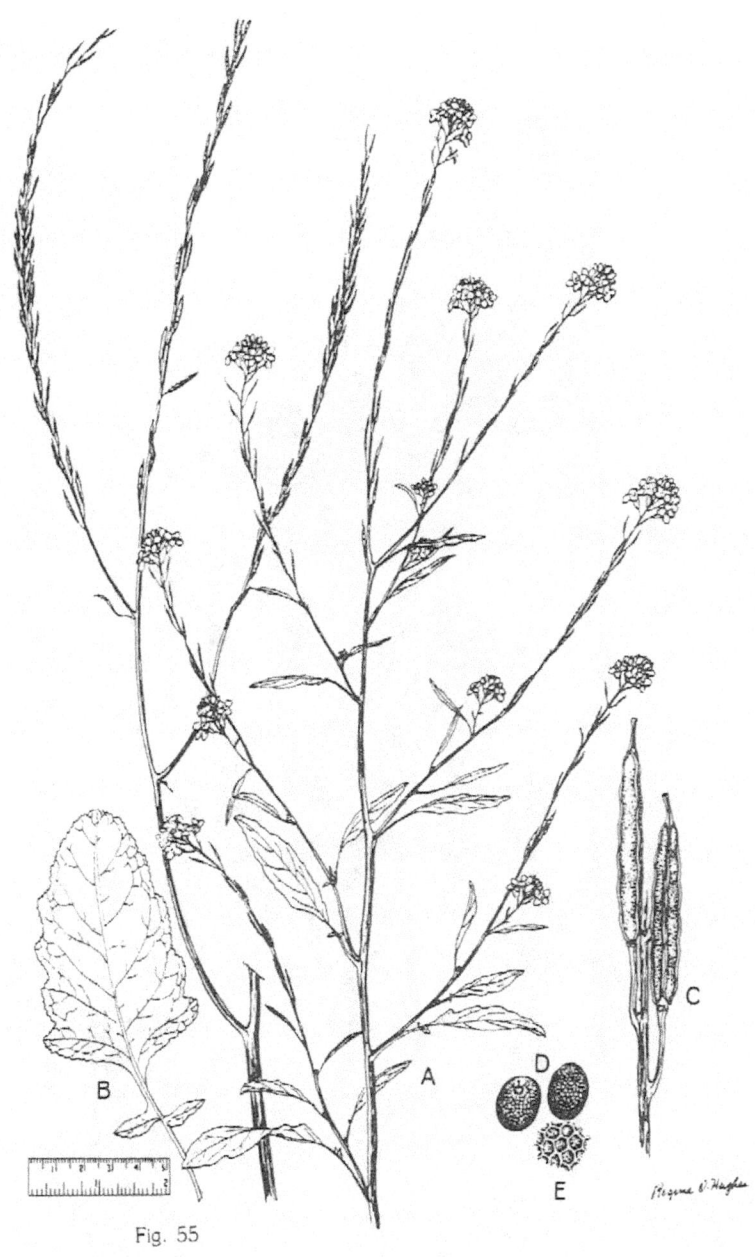

Fig. 55

BLACK MUSTARD *Brassica nigra* A. habit of growth B. basal leaf
C. seed capsule D. seeds E. reticulation pattern on seeds

Fig. 56

COMMON BURDOCK *Arctium minus* A. leaf, root, stem, fruit
B. flower C. achene

BLACK MUSTARD   *Brassica nigra*   Figure 55

The black mustard grows to a height of about five feet. It usually has a hairy stem. The lower leaves are deeply notched, the upper leaves are oblong. Flowers are bright yellow eventually producing a brown pointed seed which has a biting taste. The seeds may be ground and made into a paste for flavoring. The leaves are edible and may be cooked as greens. This plant is also listed as Sinapsis nigra.

BURDOCK   *Arctium minus*   Figure 56

This plant is easily recognized by its large rhubarb like leaves. It has a thick pulpy pithy stem. Its fruit which is burred sticks fast to clothing as well as dogs and cats. The leaves may be peeled and eaten raw or cooked. The flower stalk is also edible. The roots are edible but hard and fibrous and are made more palatable by peeling before preparation. When in bloom the flowers are small reddish violet discs surrounded by hooked bracts. The name clotbur is sometimes given to this plant.

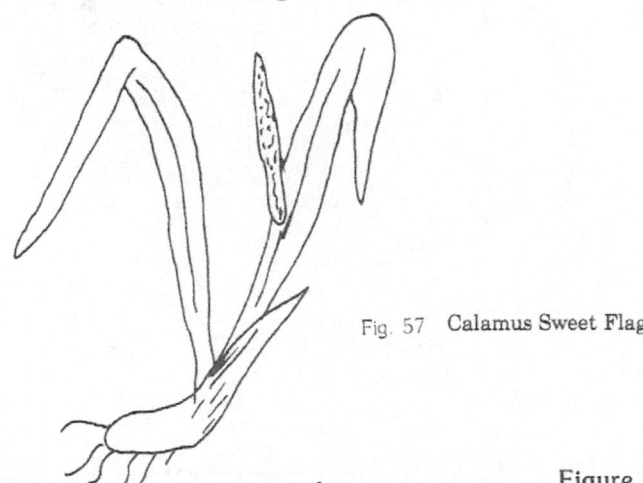

Fig. 57   Calamus Sweet Flag

CALAMUS   *Acorus calamus*   Figure 57

The calamus is also known as sweet flag, it resembles the Iris. Its leaves are greenish yellow, its flowers small. The flowers form a spike growing out of the side of a leaf like stalk. The leaves get to be three feet long in large specimens and grow from a closely packed base. The edible root has a ginger or pepper quality to it and may be candied. To candy the root, cut it into thin slices and boil in a thick syrup. Some commercial candies are made from this plant.

Fig. 58

COMMON MALLOW *Malva neglecta* A. habit B. enlarged branch
C. flower D. seed coat E. seeds

CHEESES   *Malva neglecta*   Figure 58

This plant, also known as mallow, grows in waste lands as well
as cultivated gardens. The flat leaves are edible and can be
cooked as greens or used in soups. The scalloped fruits can be
eaten raw.

Fig. 59

COMMON CHICKWEED *Stellaria media* A. habit of growth
B. flower C. seed capsule D. seeds

Fig. 60

CHICORY *Chichorium intybus*   A. habit of growth B. terminal flowers
C. involucre D. flower

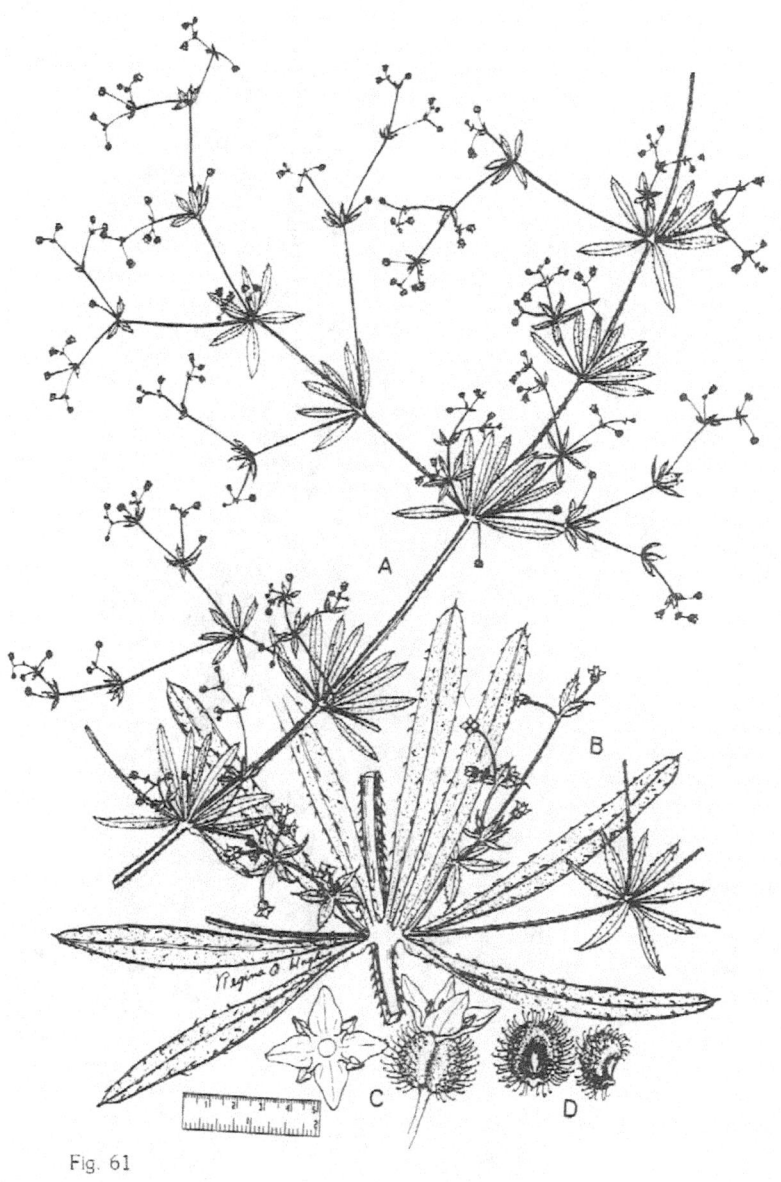

Fig. 61

CATCHWEED BEDSTRAW *Galium aparine* A. growth habit
B. enlarge leaf whorl C. flowers D. fruits

Fig. 62

COCKLEBUR *Xanthium pensylvanicum* A. habit of growth B. seedling C. bur D. seed

CHICKWEED   *Stellaria media*   Figure 59

Chickweed may be found in any season of the year around lawns and in cultivated gardens as well as along roadsides. It is found in bunches and clusters of the stems illustrated. Its stems are weak and reclining with leaves opposite each other. The flowers are small and are borne in terminal leafy clusters. The seeds are edible and the plant may be used as a cooked green.

CHICORY   *Cichorium intybus*   Figure 60

The leaves of the chicory are clustered at the top of a strong taproot. These resemble the dandelion but are thicker and tougher. The plant is best identified by its blue flowers which are sometimes referred to as corn flowers. The plant is found in fields and especially along roadsides and in waste places. Its leaves may be used as a salad green, its roots may be boiled and eaten. The root may be dried and pulverized and used as a coffee substitute. Young tender leaves may be forced from old roots by watering.

CLEAVERS   *Galium aparine*   Figure 61

Cleavers are named because of the little green balls which cling to cloth and fur. It is also called goose grass and bedstraw. The stems are long and vinelike, the leaves thin. Cleavers grow in woods covering the ground as a green mat. Use it as a cooked green, dry the seeds and make a coffee, dry the plant and make a tea.

COCKLEBUR   *Xanthium pensylvanicum*   Figure 62

This burweed has its sharp pointed fruits close to the central stem. It is a native of waste places and roadsides. Its leaves and shoots may be used as cooked greens. There is some disagreement as to the edibility of the attractive seeds. To be safe, do not eat the seeds.

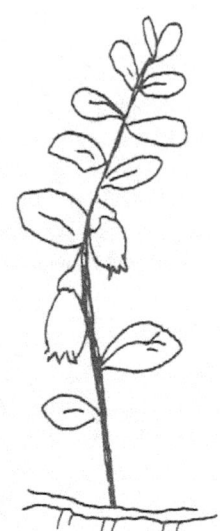

Fig. 63   Coltsfoot

Fig. 64   Snowberry

COLTSFOOT   *Tussilago farfara*   Figure 63

The coltsfoot is recognized by its yellow club like flowers which bloom before the leaves appear. It has a fleshy stem. The coltsfoot is found along new roadcuts and in other areas of damp clay. Its leaves may be dried and then slowly burned, the ashes being used for a tasty seasoning. Extracts of this plant are used in making a cough medicine called coltsfoot candy.

CLOVER

RED CLOVER   *Trifolium pratense*
SWEET CLOVER   *Melilotus officinalis*
WHITE CLOVER   *Trifolium repens*
YELLOW CLOVER *Trifolium agrarium*

The seeds and flower heads of the clovers are edible. Use these in salads. I have eaten the leaves of clovers and found them difficult to digest.

**CREEPING
SNOWBERRY**   *Chiogenes hispidula*   Figure 64

This trailing vine has the flavor of wintergreen, its berries are white and covered with small hairs. The berry is found on the lower sides of the vine like branches. The berries are edible raw or cooked.

Fig. 65

YELLOW ROCKET *Barbarea vulgaris* A. habit of growth B. flower
C. raceme of fruits D. seed capsule E. seeds

Fig. 66

WATERCRESS *Nasturtium officinale* A. habit of growth B. mature
plant C. flower D. seed capsule E. seeds

Fig. 67

FIELD PENNYCRESS   *Thlaspi arvense*   A. habit of growth B. seed coat C. seeds

Fig. 68

DANDELION *Taraxacum officinale* A. habit of growth B. flower
C. seeds D. seeds with fringe called pappus

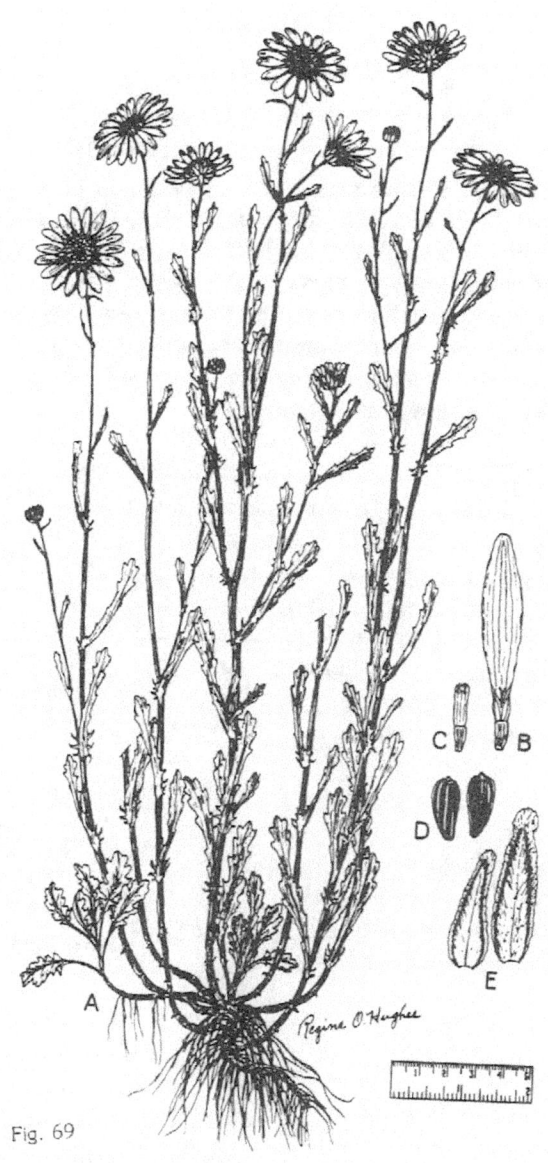

Fig. 69

OX EYE DAISY *Chrysanthemum leucanthemum* A. habit of growth
B. ray flower C. seeds D. involucral bracts

CRESS

Figure 67
Figure 66
Figure 65

PENNY CRESS   *Thlaspi arvense*

WATER CRESS   *Nasturtium officinale*

WINTER CRESS   *Barbarea vulgaris*

The various cress plants grow in large clumps of bright green leaves which remain fresh for a long time, the winter cress being available all winter. The leaf terminus is rounded. The stem is stout and shoots up early in the spring and bears elongating clusters of yellow flowers in the winter cress. Cress is found in low ground near streams and in inhabited areas. The plant is especially good in spring. Use it as a salad green, as cooked greens, or as an ingredient in soup.

DANDELION   *Taraxacum officinale*   Figure 68

The Yellow flowers of the dandelion are familiar to everyone, especially to lawn fanciers as they try to get at the flowers before they go to seed. Some dandelions are brown seeded and some are red seeded. They all have long fleshy taproots which may be dried and pulverized to make a palatable coffee. The young leaves may be used as either salad greens or cooked greens. The green leaves may be used for making a tea. The blossoms are used for making wine.

DAISY   *Chrysanthemum leucanthemum*   Figure 69

The white daisy or ox eye daisy is familiar to everyone. It is a composite flower with aggressive roots and is found in dry fields. It is smelly and to eat its edible leaves one must acquire a taste for its odor. The leaves may be used as cooked greens; the odor becomes less noticeable after a few eatings.

DAYFLOWER   *Commelina communis*   Figure 70

The dayflower has a small blue flower consisting of one pale petal and two dark petals. It grows rapidly in a sprawling manner. The leaves are parallel veined. The plant is found in shaded areas or woodlands and hedge rows. It is a frequent visitor to domestic gardens. The plant may be cooked and served as greens. Other names for it are the common dayflower and spreading dayflower.

Fig. 70   Dayflower

Fig. 71   Evening Primrose

DOCK   Figure 74

CURLED DOCK   *Rumex crispus*   Figure 72

This is a perennial plant with a large thick taproot. It has lance shaped leaves which are wavy or curled at the margins. It bears small greenish flowers which are borne in ascending fashion. The fruit at the top of the plant is reddish brown when ripe and resembles coffee grounds. The new leaves of this and all docks are wholesome and may be used as cooked greens. The plant loses much of its bulk when cooked and so ample collecting must be made to assure a mess.

SOUR DOCK   *Rumex acetosella*   Figure 73

This sour dock is easily recognized by its arrowhead like leaves containing a sour juice, hence also the name sorrel and chow chow. The branching stalks of tiny flowers are followed by tiny seeds. The seed stalks develop the second year. The male flowers are yellowish and the female flowers are reddish brown. This plant is a sign of acid soil and is found in fields and lawns and on the edges of properties. Use the leaves in green salads, cook them as greens, or simmer the leaves in water to make a hot or cold lemonade.

Fig. 72

CURLY DOCK *Rumex crispus* A. habit of growth B. fruit C. seed

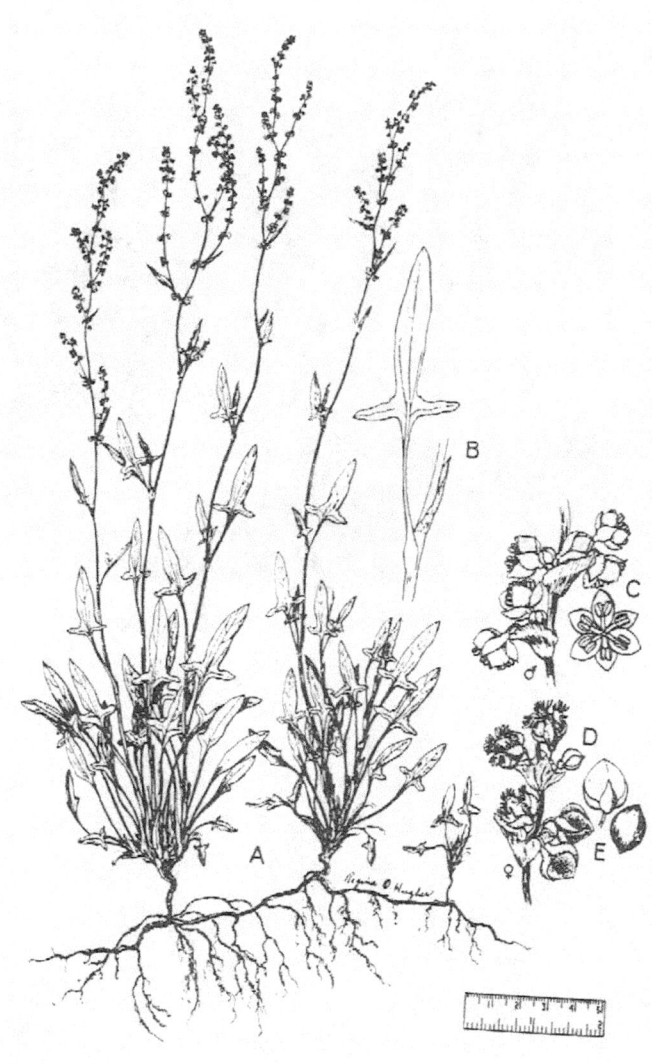

Fig. 73

RED SORREL *Rumex acetosella* A. growth habit B. leaf detail
C. staminate flowers D. pistillate flowers E. achenes or seeds

Figure 74: Broad leaf dock, *Rumex*

**EVENING
PRIMROSE**   *Oenothera biennis*   Figure 71

The mature primrose stands from two to four feet high with flowers about an inch in diameter which open in late afternoon. The flowers which appear in the second year are blunt and light yellow in color. The leaves are elliptical with sparsely toothed margins. It is found in thickets and other dry habitats. The leaves of the young plant are palatable peeled and eaten raw. The root may be used as a vegetable and is excellent in stews.

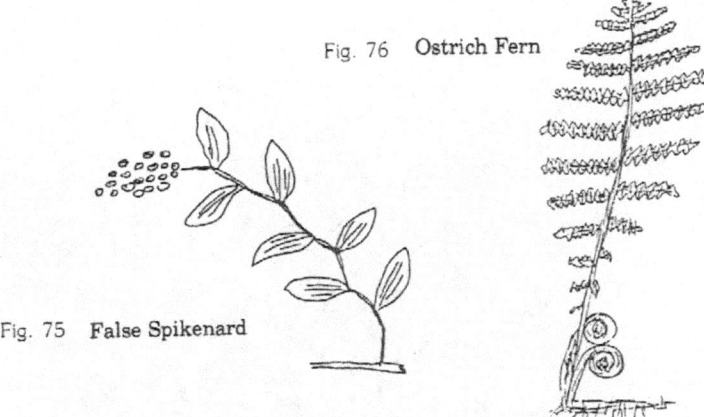

Fig. 76 Ostrich Fern

Fig. 75 False Spikenard

FALSE SPIKENARD   *Smilacina racemosa*   Figure 75

This false Solomon's Seal or Solomon's Plume produces an edible reddish berry in the fall. It does not have the underground stem system of the real Solomon's Seal, hence its name. Its numerous leaves are hairy edged and veiny. It reaches a height of about two feet. It is sometimes listed as plume lily in reference works.

FERN

BRACKEN FERN   *Pteris aquilina*   Figure 77

This is a coarse fern with solitary or scattered young stalks. Its base is covered with rusty felt and has an extensive creeping rootstalk. It is found in open woods and pastures. The young fronds are edible when unrolled. Young shoots may be cooked and eaten, the roots or rhizomes may also be boiled and eaten or dried and made into meal and then into bread. The plant can also be used to make a good beer.

OSTRICH FERN   *Matteuccia struthiopteris*   Figure 76

The young fronds of this fern form dense vaselike clumps which rise from a free forking rootstock. Last years fronds resemble thick dark brown feathers, the new fronds bear brown scales with a feather like leafy summit. The leaves of this plant look like ostrich feathers, hence the name. The new leaves rise from circular clumps which look like fiddleheads. These fiddleheads are edible raw or cooked. Boil them in salt water and serve with bacon drippings. Check out stream beds and rich woods for this fern in the fall and mark the spot well, return in spring and begin your harvest.

Fig. 77

BRACKEN *Pteridium aquilinum* A. habit of growth B. pinnules showing marginal sori C. nectary glands

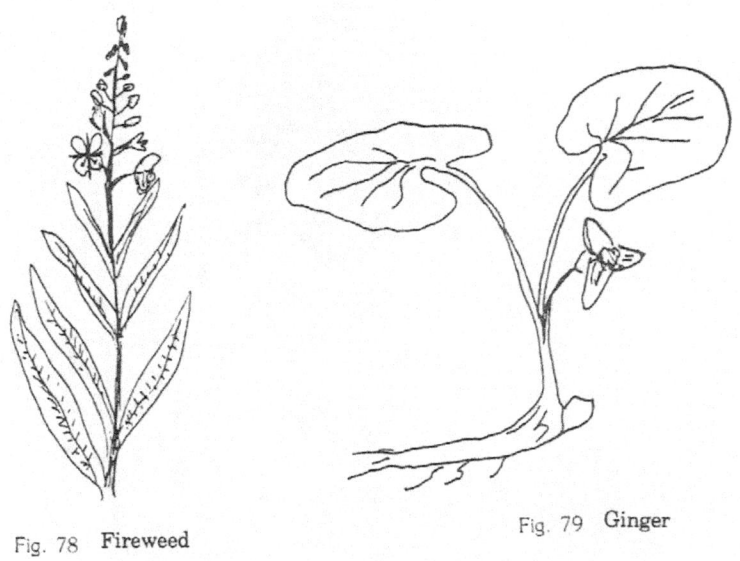

Fig. 78   Fireweed

Fig. 79   Ginger

FIREWEED   *Epilobium angustifolium*   Figure 78

The fireweed grows to a height of three to five feet. Its flowers are about an inch in diameter and are bright purple in color. The fireweed seeds bear long white hairs. The plant is found in open woods and thickets and is abundant in burnt over areas from which it gets its name. Use the leaves for tea or boil the leaves and stems for cooked greens. The plant may be dried and used as an herb.

GINGER   *Asarum canadense*   Figure 79

The wild ginger plant appears as a two leaved plant with the leaves flattening out at the top of the stem. The leaves are heart shaped and about five inches wide. This woodland plant bears a solitary three pointed brownish purple flower. The root has a strong ginger flavor and can be munched on raw or boiled with brown sugar and preserved as a candy. The root can be added to stews or used in other forms of cooking. A tea can be made from the root by boiling only a few minutes.

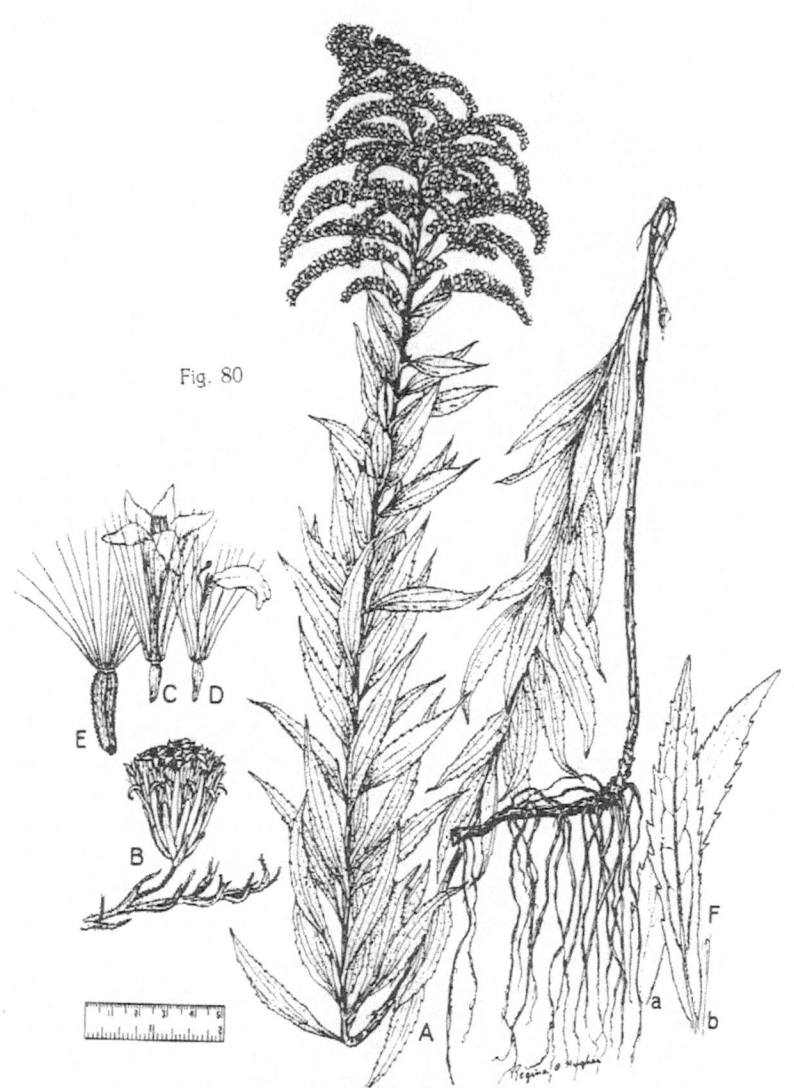

Fig. 80

CANADA GOLDENROD *Solidago canadensis* A. habit of growth
B. flower head C. disk flower D. ray flower E. seed F. leaves

GOLDENROD *Solidago odora*

The sweet goldenrod is a slender plant reaching three feet in
height. Its flowers are yellowish and tend to be on one side
of the plant. Its leaves are narrow and dotted with small glands
which yield a pleasant odor. Either the dried seed heads or the
dried leaves will make an acceptable tea, or both together.

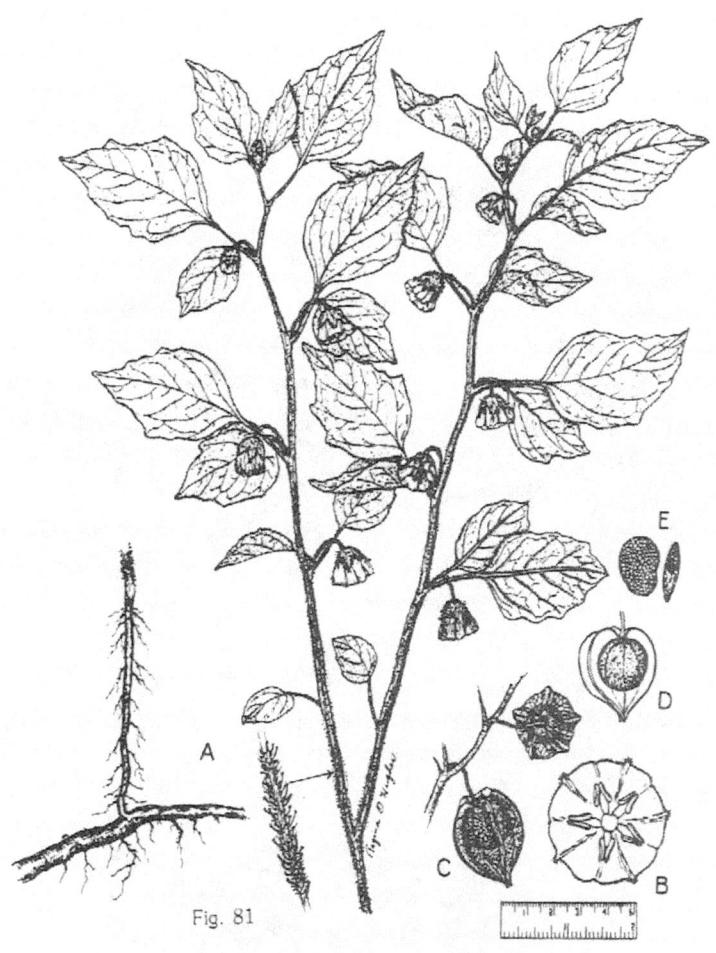

Fig. 81

CLAMMY GROUNDCHERRY *Physalis hetrophylla* A. habit of growth B. flower open C. berries in case D. fruit showing berry E. seeds

GROUND CHERRY   *Physalis species*   Figure 81

The ground cherry grows to about a foot in height but its drooping nature gives one the impression that it is much bigger. Its fruit is easily recognized being a cherry or small tomato encased in a lantern like paper husk, hence it is known as Chinese or Japanese lantern as well as husk tomato. The cherry may be eaten raw or cooked or put in preserves. It is worth seeking and tasting.

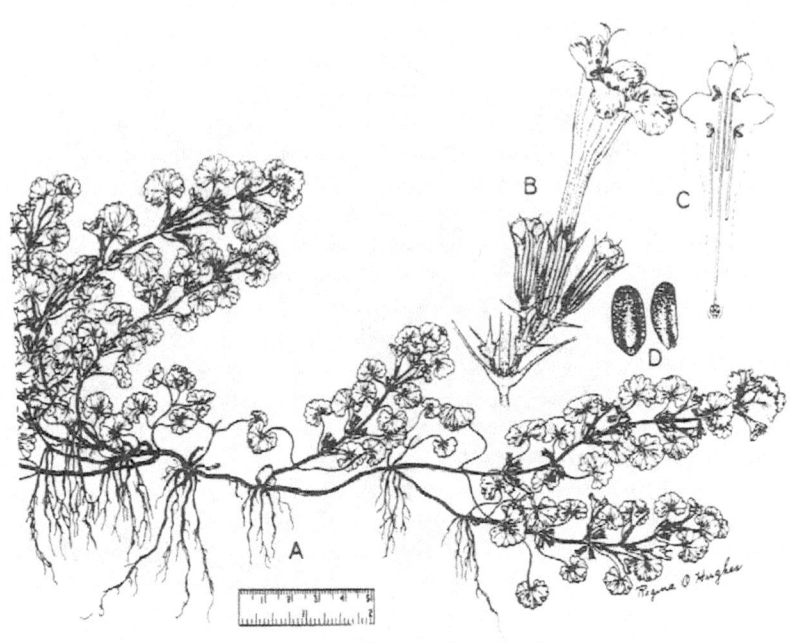

Fig. 82

GROUND IVY *Glechoma hederacea* A. habit of growth B. flower
C. flower diagram D. seeds

GROUND IVY   *Glechoma hederacea*   Figure 82

This creeping member of the mint family forms mats along hedge
rows. It is also known as Gill Over The Ground. Its flowers
are small and lavender. The leaves of ground ivy are round
with blunt tooth edges; these may be dried and used to make

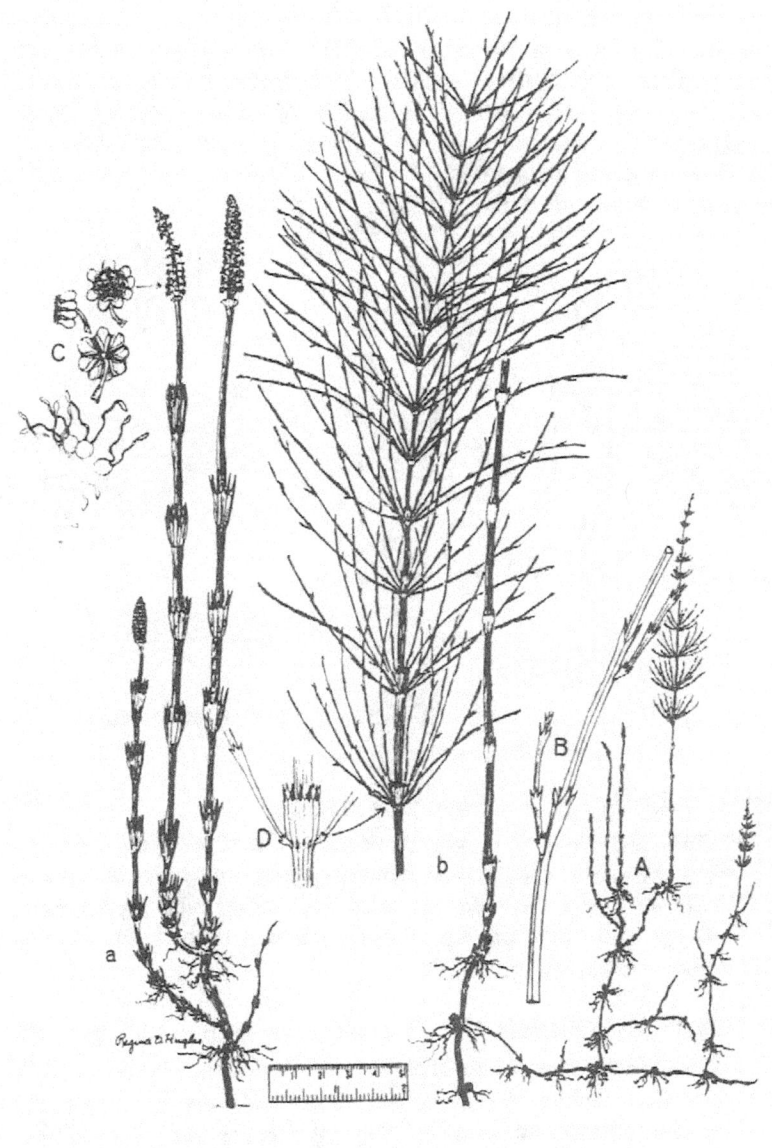

Fig. 83

HORSETAIL *Equisetum arvense* A. habit of growth B. enlarged
branch C. sporangiophores D. sheath E. spores

HONEWORT   *Cryptotaenia canadensis*   Figure 84

The five petaled flowers of the honewort are small and incon-
spicuous. Its fruit is composed of dry seeds and its leaves are
long stalked with coarse toothing. The dry seeds are about an
inch long and split into halves easily. It is a native of moist
woodlands. The leaves may be used as greens and in soups.
The root is edible and should be cooked. Stems and leaves may
be used in salads or dried as an herb.

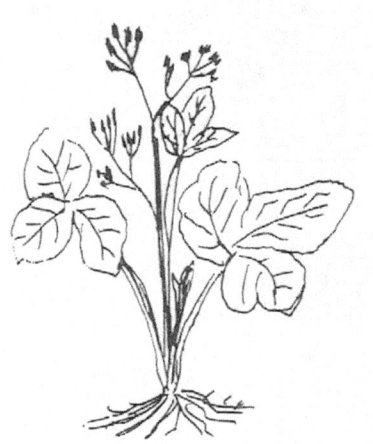

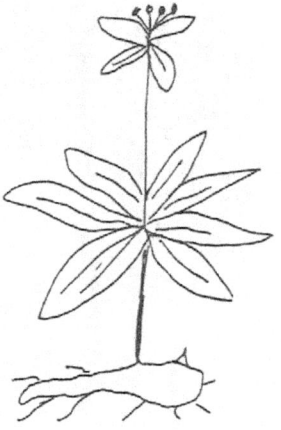

Fig. 85   Indian Cucumber

Fig. 84   Honewort

HORSETAIL   *Equisetum arvense*   Figure 83

This pipe joint grass is easily recognized. It and its relative
the scouring rush, *Equisetum hyemale,* may be cooked as greens
when young. The shoots may also be peeled and eaten raw.
Do not use the older plants or plants which have been cut for
more than a day for food.

INDIAN CUCUMBER   *Medeola virginiana*   Figure 85

The Indian Cucumber is a single stemmed woodland plant which
stands erect. It has a rosette of leaves halfway up the stem
and another smaller set near the top. In autumn the green leaves
become purplish. The pale yellow flowers near the apex of the
stalk become purple black berries in the fall. The long white
brittle crispy roots are edible raw or cooked. It is delicious raw
and it is easy to extract with little digging. It may be gathered
at any time but may be difficult to find in the winter when
the leaves disappear.

Fig. 86

LAMBS QUARTERS *Chenopoduim album* A. habit of growth
B. floral spike C. flowers D. seed holder E. seed

JEWEL WEED   *Impatiens biflora*

The spotted touch me not or snapweed has orange flowers with purple spots. If you touch it when mature it will shoot out its seeds. When young, the stems are edible as cooked greens or raw for its high moisture content.

KNOTWEED   *Polygonum cuspidatum*   Figure 87

The Japanese Knotweed is an erect shrub reaching to eight feet in height. It is recognized by its similarity to bamboo. Its leaves are stalked and eggshaped with a squared base. Its flowers are greenish white. It is found in waste places along roadsides, and on once inhabited land. The young leaves may be used as a salad green or cooked green. The roots may be cooked and eaten at any season of the year. Even though it is of shrub quality since it grows new shoots each year it is placed in this section of low plants.

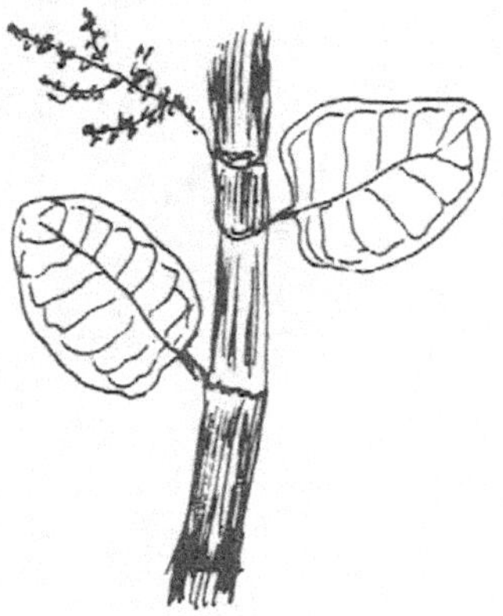

Fig. 87   Knotweed

LAMB'S QUARTERS   *Chenopodium album*   Figure 86

The leaves of lamb's quarters are alternate and long stemmed with angular toothing especially near the base. When picking the leaves one will notice the mealy character of the undersides. Older plants bear scalloped green flowers in clusters which turn to small black seeds. The lower leaves of the plant often have purple blotches caused by a fungus. The plant is found as a weed in almost all gardens, around buildings, and in roadside situations. It is a delicious plant when boiled as greens. The seeds are edible and may be pounded into meal. Avoid the leaves tainted with the red or violet fungus. The orach, Atriplex sp., resembles lamb's quarters and is easily mistaken for it. It is a common plant of the seacoasts and delicious as a cooked green. It has a slightly salt taste and is therefore referred to as saltbush.

Figure 88: Marsh Marigold, *Caltha palustris*

Figure 89: Mayapple, *Podophyllum peltatum*

MARSH MARIGOLD *Caltha palustris* Figure 88

The leaves of this cowslip are kidney shaped, scalloped around the edges and edible. They and the young stems may be used as cooked greens. The flowers of the plant are orange yellow and are found in leafy clusters on hollow stems. The plant is native to wet meadows and swamps, hence its other name of meadow bright. Besides the edible leaves and stems the flower buds may be pickled. Absolutely do not eat the plant raw.

MAYAPPLE *Podophyllum peltatum* Figure 89

This plant, also known as mandrake, is recognized by its umbrella like stance in woodlands. Its flower is white and large, being carried between the forks of the two large leaves. The apple is a yellow berry. The leaves are deeply divided into coarse toothed lobes. Use the apple raw or in jellies. The fruit is ripe when it is yellow. Do not eat the leaves or the roots since they are poisonous.

MILKWEED *Asclepias syriaca* Figure 90

The milkweed or silkweed is common and easily recognized by its milky juice. Its leaves are broad and oblong, its flowers are showy and near the middle of summer turn into little pods which when mature produce a silken seed. The milkweed is found in open places, along fence rows, and along roadsides. The new tender shoots may be used as cooked greens, the young pods may be eaten raw or cooked. The pods which have a nutty flavor are excellent with meat. The flower buds may be cooked, these are claimed by many to be the most tasty part of the plant.

MINT *Mentha candensis*
PEPPERMINT *Mentha piperita*
SPEARMINT *Mentha spicata*

Mints have square stems and opposite leaves which contain a fragrant oil. The plant oil can be used for flavoring. Leaves may be roasted or eaten directly. A bit of salt sets the flavor off nicely. Boil the leaves for mint tea or dry them for herb use. Pennyroyal, Hedeoma sp., is a mint used in making tea. It is found in dry fields and is well known in many localities.

Fig. 90

COMMON MILKWEED *Ascelepias syriaca* A. habit of growth
B. flower C. follicles D. seeds with fringe

Fig. 91

BLACK NIGHTSHADE *Solanum nigrum* A. habit of growth B. flower arrangement C. seeds

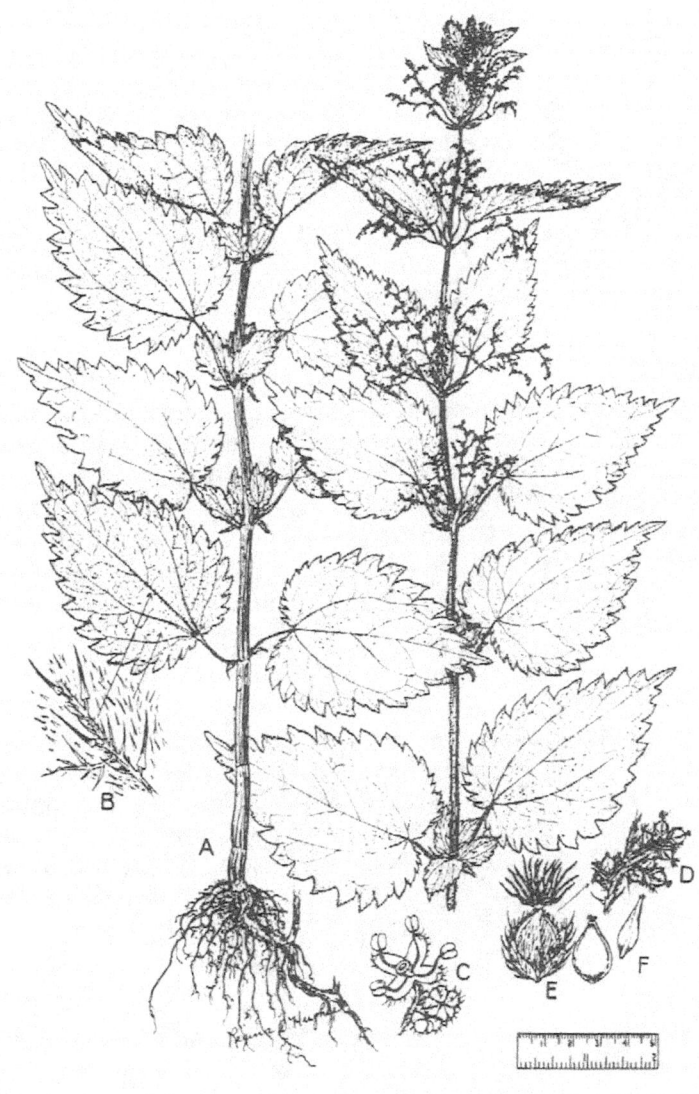

Fig. 92

STINGING NEEDLE *Urtica dioica* A. habit of growth B. stinging hairs
enlarged C. flowers D. fruit spike E. fruit F. seeds

BLACK NIGHTSHADE   *Solanum nigrum*   Figure 91

This is a low branched and spreading annual which bears small white flowers in clusters. It may be described as bushy branched. It is found in dry open soil, at the borders of woods, along roadsides, and on cultivated land. The berries are black and may be made into pies or eaten raw. The young shoots and leaves are also edible. Do not confuse this plant with the climbing nightshade, also known as the deadly nightshade, whose berries are toxic but not necessarily as fatal as the name implies. The berries of the deadly nightshade are red and should be avoided. Don't eat either plant unless you are sure of its identity.

NETTLE   *Urtica species*   Figure 92

The nettles are erect plants with coarsely toothed strongly ribbed leaves. The lower leaves are covered with fine stinging bristles. The flowers which are borne in small greenish clusters are found in the upper axils of the plant in summer. The leaves may be collected with gloves to prevent getting stung. They are excellent as cooked greens, cook for about five minutes, do not overcook them. The leaves loose their stinging quality upon cooking. Especially good is the stinging nettle, *Urtica dioica*.

WILD ONION   *Allium cernuum*   Figure 93

There are many names for the wild onion and many varieties of the basic form. All forms have a bulb at the base with tubular leaves. The flowers are pinkish white. Plants of this nature have been also called wild garlic, wild leek, meadow garlic, and field garlic. Use these in soups and stews. If you eat it raw it will taste good and strong for the moment as well as days later. The plant can be dried and stored for future use.

ORPINE   *Sedum telephium*   Figure 96

This weed grows to about two feet in height and bears succulent leaves crowded spirally around a stem. Its flowers are small and are from reddish to white. It has fleshy tuber like roots and is native of damp fields, roadsides, and other weed habitats. It can be used as a salad green while young. The leaves and stems can also be used as a cooked green. The roots or tubers may be boiled and served with salt and a dash of vinegar or pickled for future use.

Fig. 93

WILD ONION *Allium vineale* A. habit of growth B. flower cluster
C. bulblets D. flower E. bulbs F. bulbs without shell

Fig. 94

WOOD SORREL *Oxalis stricta* A. habit of growth B. enlarged leave
C. flower D. capsule E. seeds

OXALIS *Oxalis species* Figure 94

This sour grass is found around your yard as well as in the
woods. It has clover like leaves which are notched. The flowers
have five petals and are yellow in the species above. Other edible
species have white or pink petals. The whole plant is acid to
the taste, hence its other name of wood sorrel. Use it raw in
salads. The onion like tubers may be eaten raw or boiled.

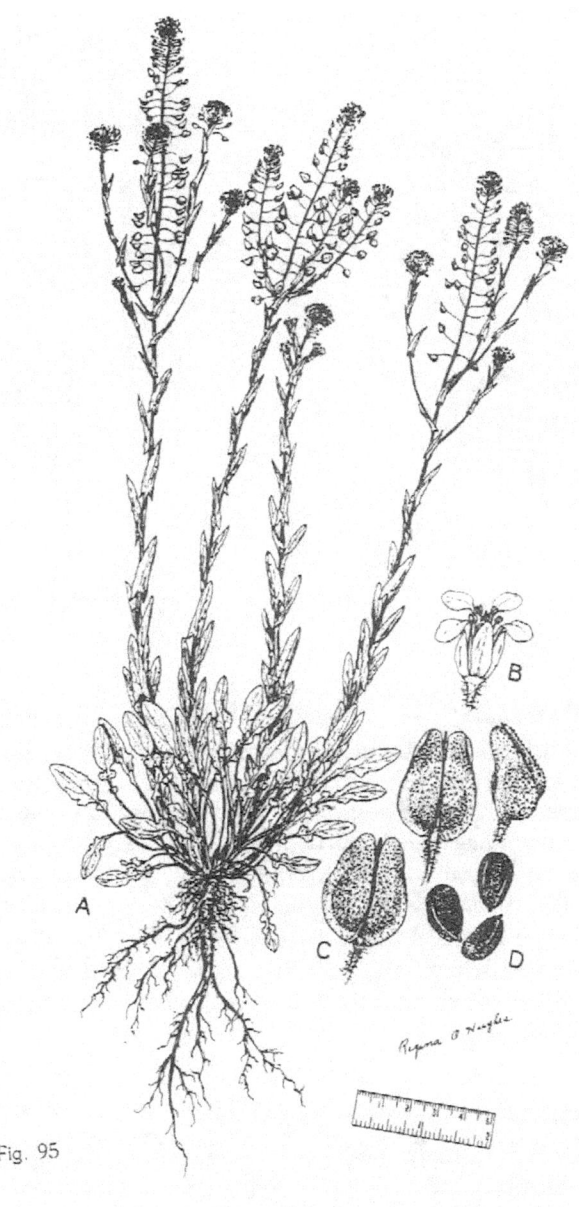

Fig. 95

FIELD PEPPERWEED *Lepidium campestre* A. habit of growth
B. flower C. seed coating D. seeds

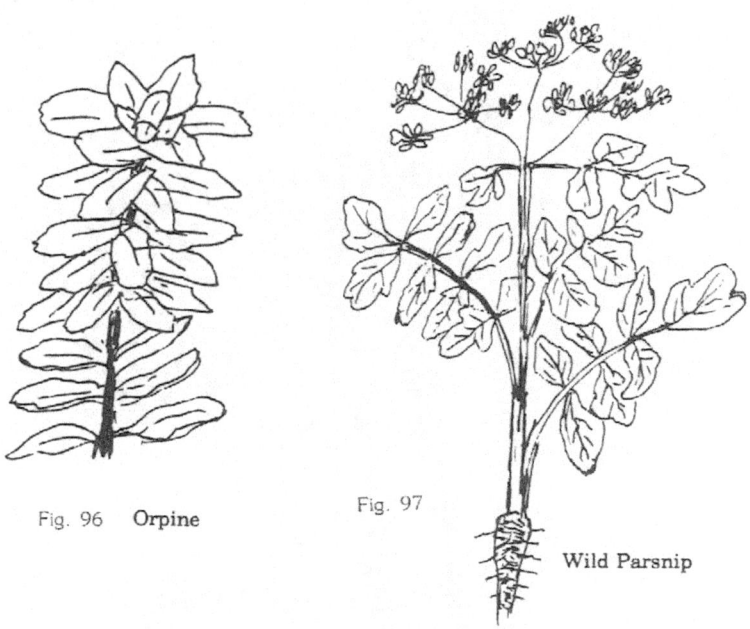

Fig. 96   Orpine

Fig. 97

Wild Parsnip

PARSNIP (WILD)   *Pastinaca sativa*   Figure 97

This is the wild form of the cultivated parsnip. It is identified by its tall hollow branching stem which is deeply grooved all the way to its tip. The leaves are pinnately compound and coarsely toothed with lobed segments. The flowers are small and yellow and are in large compound flat topped groups. The seeds are flattened. The plant and seeds have a distinct unpleasant odor. Wild parsnips are found along roadways, railroad beds, and formerly cultivated areas. The root is a taproot, long and narrow and it is edible raw or cooked. See notes on water hemlock and poison hemlock also.

PEPPERGRASS   *Lepidium virginicum*   Figure 95

Peppergrass leaves form rosettes in spring and are cress like. They bear minute white flowers in spike like clusters. Seed pods are flat, circular, and similar to shepherd's purse seeds in growth pattern. Use as a salad green or as a garnish. The seeds are tasty.

Fig. 98

GREEN AMARANTH (REDROOT) *Amarantus retroflexus* A. habit
of growth B. spikelet C. seed capsule D. seeds

PIGWEED   *Amaranthus retroflexus*   Figure 98

The seeds and flowers of the *amaranth* have a strawlike character. Its leaves and stems are often hairy. This plant is found in the garden as a weed and can usually be identified by its red roots, hence also the name of redroot. I prefer the name *amaranth* or green *amaranth* by which it is also known since pigweed is not savory and the plant is one of the most delicious of the wild ones. The seeds are edible and the young shoots and leaves may be eaten as a cooked green.

PLANTAIN   *Plantago major*   Figure 99

This is the common dooryard plantain which has broad leaves and strong stringy fibers in them. In spring the young leaves may be used as cooked greens. Regardless of preparation the plant is tough and if eaten raw causes indigestion in the strongest of stomachs.

POKEWEED   *Phytolacca americana*   Figure 100

The pokeweed is a tall coarse plant with elliptical pointed leaves which reach lengths of ten inches. The tall stems are tinted purple. The plant is also called inkberry by many since its fruit is in the form of dark purple berries which are found in clusters atop the stems. The pokeweed is found in open soil, in wood clearings, along roadsides, and in cultivated gardens. The young shoots may be cooked as greens. This is probably the most famous of the edible wild plants. Some prefer to throw away the first cooking water and do a second quick boiling. The fruit of poke is edible but the seeds are poisonous so do not eat the fruit. The root is poisonous and so is the older stem.

                                                    Figure 52
PURSLANE   *Portulaca oleracea*   Figure 101

This succulent is a common visitor to cultivated gardens and fields since its seeds are a common impurity in seed packets. It is a matted creeping herb with moist looking stems and very fleshy narrowly wedge shaped reddish green opposite leaves. The flowers have yellow petals. The top of the seed pod lifts off like a cap. Use the plant as cooked greens, use in soups, or pickle it. The seeds are edible. The stems may be eaten raw for their moisture but let us hope that one is never that thirsty.

Fig. 99

A. NARROW LEAF PLANTAIN *Plantago lanceolata* a. flower b. capsule c. seed

B. BROADLEAF PLANTAIN *Plantago major* a. flower b. capsule c. seeds

C. BLACKSEED PLANTAIN *Plantago rugeli* a. flower b. capsule c. seeds

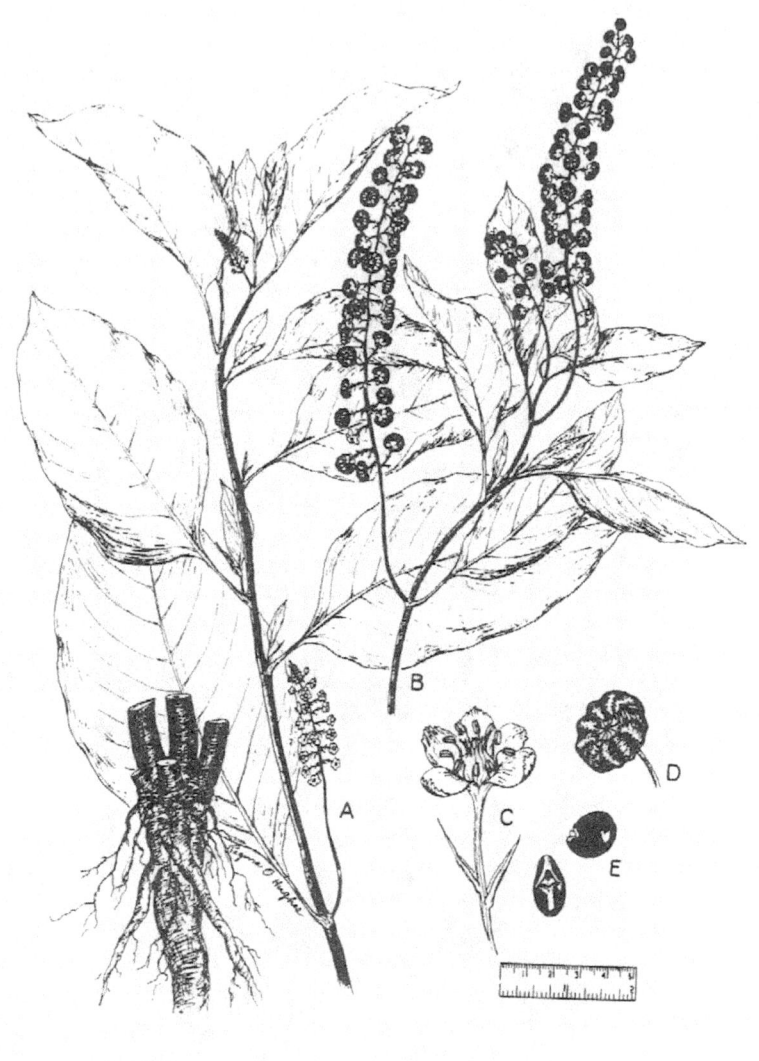

Fig. 100

POKEWEED *Phytolacca americana* A. habit of growth B. fruiting stem
C. flower D. berry E. seeds

Fig. 101

PURSLANE *Portulaca oleracea* A. habit of growth B. flowers and cap
sules C. flower open D. seeds

Fig. 102

QUACKGRASS *Agropyron repens* A. habit of growth B. spikelet
C. ligule D. florets

Fig. 103

QUEEN ANNES LACE *Daucus carota* A. habit of growth B. flowers
C. seed D. cross section of seed

QUACKGRASS *Agropyron repens* Figure 102

Quackgrass has slender wiry white roots with tenacious joints. It spreads by this creeping rhizome. Its leaves are flat and dark green. The erect stalk terminates in a finger like spike with alternate notches of spikelets. The grass is found on open ground and is considered an obnoxious weed in cultivated ground. A good bread may be prepared by drying and grinding the roots.

QUEEN ANNE'S LACE *Daucus carota* Figure 103

The bird's nest appearance of the flowers of this plant are easily recognized. The plant may grow to three feet in height with leaves cut in fernlike fashion. Flowers are compound white and usually have a purple or red flower at its center. Queen Anne's Lace is found in dry pastures and fields which are returning back to nature. The root is edible and was the source of our present domestic carrot. This plant resembles the poison water hemlock. Refer to the notes on the low hemlocks in section II.

RICE *Zizania species* Figure 105

The Indian Rice or Wild Rice is a grass of lakes and other water margins. It is similar to oats with its loose husk having a long bristle at the top. The grain is dark brown, less than an inch long, and falls from the husk when ripe so it must be gathered at the right time which is just as the grains start to fall. Its greatest abundance is in the western Great Lakes region and if a northern lake is named Rice Lake it is after this grain and not somebody named Rice. It may be cooked as you would ordinary rice.

SALSIFY *Tragopogon porrifolius* Figure 106

A milky juice is secreted from the broad grassblade leaves of this goat's beard or oyster plant. The flowering stem develops in the second year with flowers resembling large dandelions and purple in color. Closely related species which are also edible have yellow flowers. The plant is native to fields and roadsides. The roots can be eaten throughout the winter and are usually boiled or fried. New spring shoots are used as cooked greens.

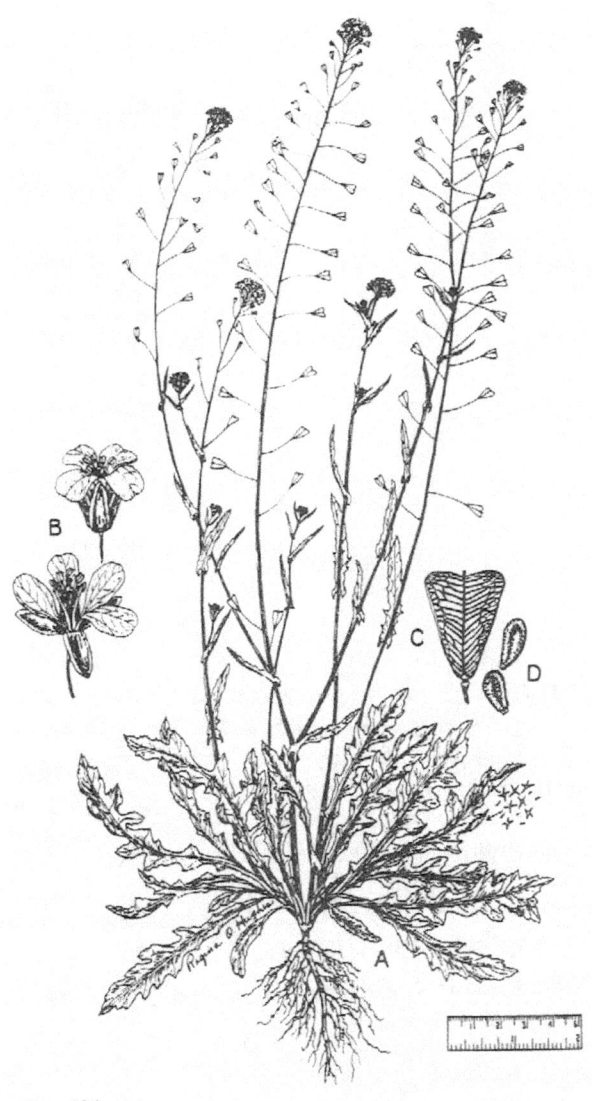

Fig. 104

SHEPERDS PURSE *Capsella bursa-pastoris* A. habit of growth
B. flowers C. seed capsule D. seeds

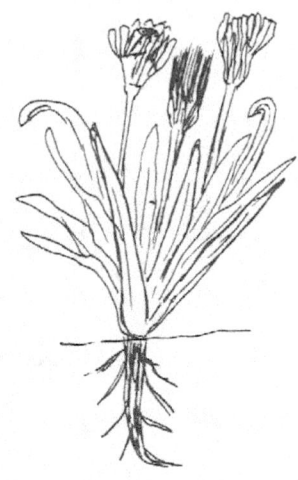

Fig. 105   Wild Rice   Fig. 106   Salsify

SHEPHERD'S
PURSE   *Capsella bursapastoris*   Figure 104

Leaves of this mustard plant are basal with various lobes as
well as sharp toothing. Its lower leaves have long tapering bases
and its stem leaves are entire with clasping bases. The flowers
are small and white growing out from the tall stems. The fruit
forms a sort of triangle. Shepherd's Purse may be found in lawns
and gardens as well as waste places and areas once occupied
by man. Use as cooked greens.

Figure 108

SOLOMON'S SEAL   *Polygonatum species*   Figure 110

Flowers of the solomon's seal are greenish white and grow on
a stalk from three to five feet high. The plant is often bent
over and it has alternate smooth leaves from the axils of which
the flowers rise. The fruit is in the form of bluish berries. The
plant gets its name from the scars on its underground stem.
It is native of the woodland. Use by boiling the young shoots
and roots. This plant is rare and should really not be used unless
there is some sort of gourmet emergency.

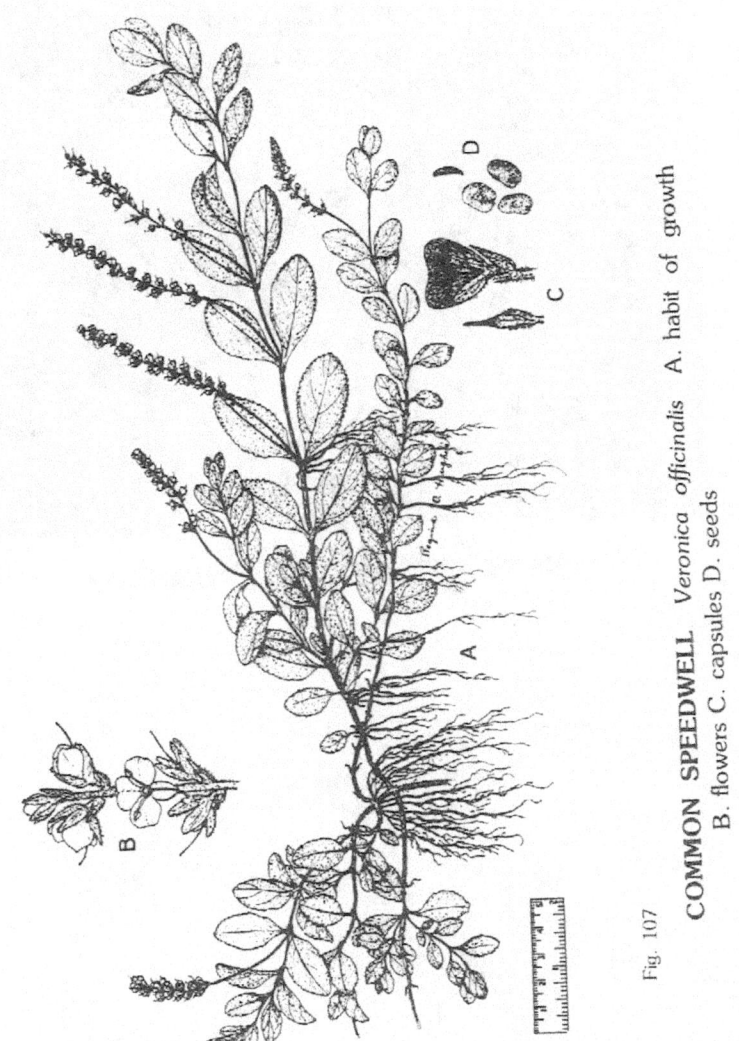

Fig. 107

COMMON SPEEDWELL *Veronica officinalis* A. habit of growth
B. flowers C. capsules D. seeds

Figure 108: Solomon Seal root, *Polygonatum*

Fig. 109 Spiderwort

Fig. 110 Solomon's Seal

SPEEDWELL   *Veronica species*   Figure 107

Speedwell is a sprawling perennial with lavender blue flowers. It is found in many varieties, especially common in bird's eye speedwell. Its leaves are broad and hairy and have coarsely rounded teeth. The leaves are opposite each other on the stems. The plant is found in dry open woods as well as on roadsides and in abandoned fields. It forms large colonies due to its trailing habit. Use the leaves for making tea.

SPIDERWORT   *Tradescantia virginica*   Figure 109

This is one of the many edible spiderworts. The flowers are radial, that is, arranged in circular fashion. Their color is violet to white. Leaves are long and narrow and appear bluish green. The plant is found in grasslands and open woods. Cook the young stems and leaves as greens.

SPRING BEAUTY   *Claytonia caroliniana*   Figure 111

This member of the portulaca family has stems several inches high which have pairs of long narrow leaves. The flowers are about a half inch in diameter and are white to pink. The root system is in the form of a tuber. The plant is found in open woods and grasslands. The bulbs or tubers are edible.

STRAWBERRY   *Fragaria virginiana*   Figure 112

The wild strawberry easily outclasses its domestic relatives in flavor. The leaves which are covered with fine hairs grow directly from the roots. They are three in number and are broad and saw toothed. The flower is white. The berries progress from green to white and then finally to beautiful red. The berry is of course, edible. The leaves may be used to brew a pleasant tea.

SUNFLOWER   Figure 113
(JERUSALEM ARTICHOKE)   *Helianthus tuberosus*

Once I had discovered the Jerusalem artichoke, *Helianthus tuberosus*, it seemed to be everywhere. These sunflowers are quite common. The tubers or roots are excellent roasted, boiled or pickled. They are found along railroad tracks, roadsides, and in waste places, look for them.

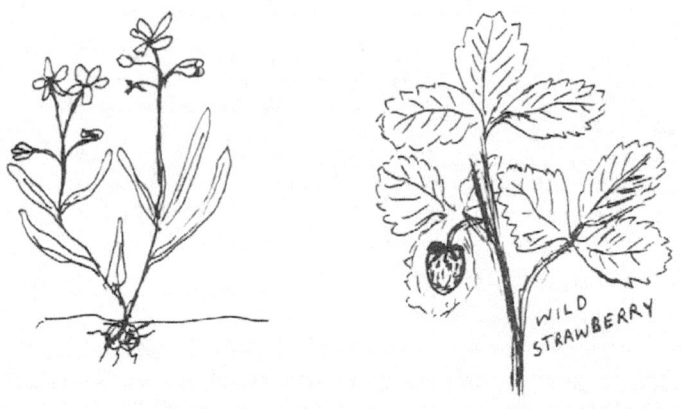

Fig. 111   Spring Beauty

Fig. 112   Strawberry

Figure 113: Jerusalem Artichoke or Sunflower, *Helianthus tuberosus*

Fig. 114   Tansy

Fig. 115   Teaberry

Figure 128

Figure 114

TANSY   *Tanacetum vulgare*   Figure 114

The tansy grows to a height of almost three feet in good soil but is usually found to be about a foot and a half tall. It is perennial and the flower heads are numerous with a flat topped grouping. The flowers are yellow. The leaves of the tansy are large and divided in a fern type pattern. The plant is found mostly in once lived in areas and is most easily recognized by its yellow button heads. The plant is highly aromatic and has been used in folk medicine for centuries. Use it as an herb or to make a bitter tea.

TEABERRY   *Gaultheria procumbens*   Figure 115

This wintergreen is a low plant creeping beneath other foliage near the ground surface. It has erect branches from three to six inches high. The aromatic leaves which are rigid or stiff are colored dark glossy green. The oval leaves have small bristle tipped teeth. The red berry hangs on the stem all winter. The plant is found in hilly and mountainous surroundings frequently in association with evergreens. The berry may be eaten raw or used in cooked dishes. A tea may be prepared from the leaves.

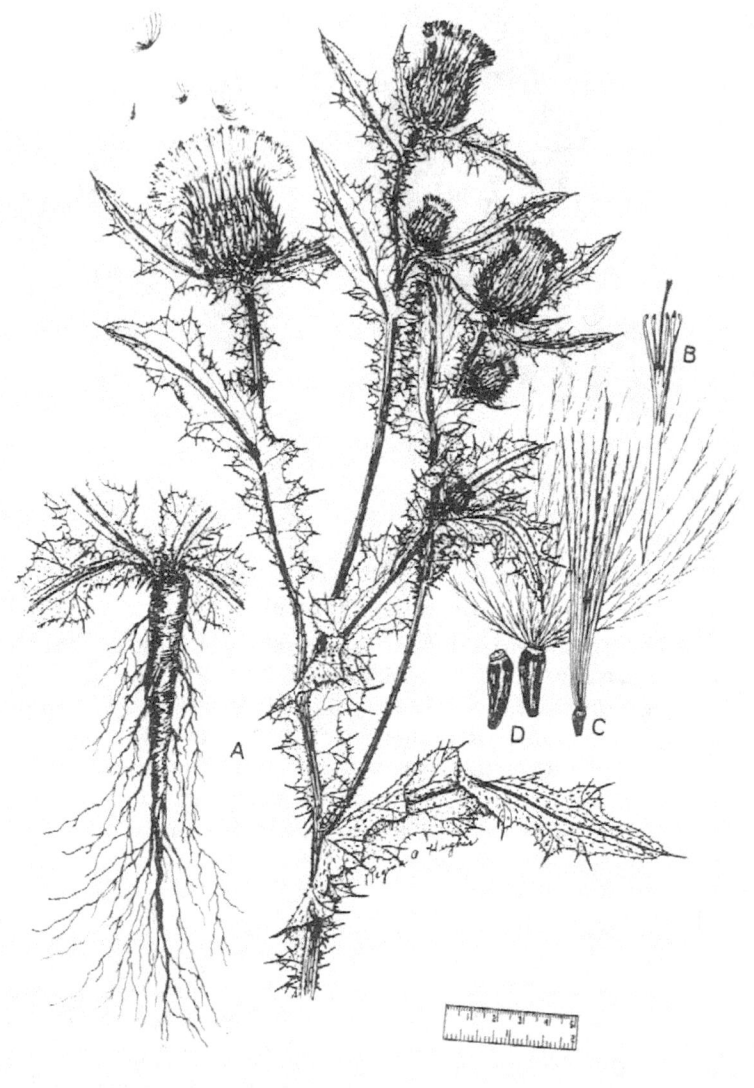

Fig. 116

BULL THISTLE *Cirsium vulgare* A. habit of growth B. flower C. immature fruit D. seeds

Fig. 117

SOWTHISTLE *Sonchus oleraceus* A. habit of growth B. flower head
C. ray flower D. achenes or seeds with flight pappus

THISTLE

COMMON THISTLE
(JOHNNY GREEN)   *Cirsium vulgare*   Figure 116

Remove thorns from the leaves and eat raw or cooked. The stalk may be peeled and also eaten raw or cooked.

SOW THISTLE   *Sonchus species*   Figure 117

This coarse prickly plant grows to a height of four feet. Its leaves have prickly margins and are often prominently lobed. The flowers are bright yellow. The plant secretes a milky bitter juice. It is found as a weed in cultivated land and along roadsides. Use only young and tender plants as a salad green or cooked green.

STAR THISTLE   *Centaurea species*

The young stems and leaves may be eaten raw or cooked on both the sow and star thistles.

TOOTHWORTS   *Dentaria species*

The cut leaved toothwort, *Dentaria laciniata* and the two leaved toothwort, *Dentaria diphylla,* are members of the mustard family. The roots are mustardy and hence the name pepperroots. The edible roots are toothed or highly crinkled and may be used as a relish.

VETCH   *Vicia species*   Figure 119

The vetch is a member of the pea family and has the same tendril climbing habit originating at the tip of its pinnate leaves. The vetch flowers are slightly less than an inch long and are found in sparse groups. They are purple. It is a plant of moist woodlands and tall brush. The seeds are edible and can be used in soups or in breads much the same as caraway seeds.

YELLOW ADDER'S
TONGUE   *Erythronium americanum*   Figure 120

The fawn lily or trout lily rises as a single flower stalk bearing a yellow bell shaped flower. Its leaves are two or three, elliptical and deeply mottled. It is a native of woodlands. Use the bulbous root as a cooked vegetable. Use the leaves as cooked greens.

Fig. 118

YELLOW NUTSEDGE *Cyperus esculentus* A. habit of growth
B. spikelet C. seeds

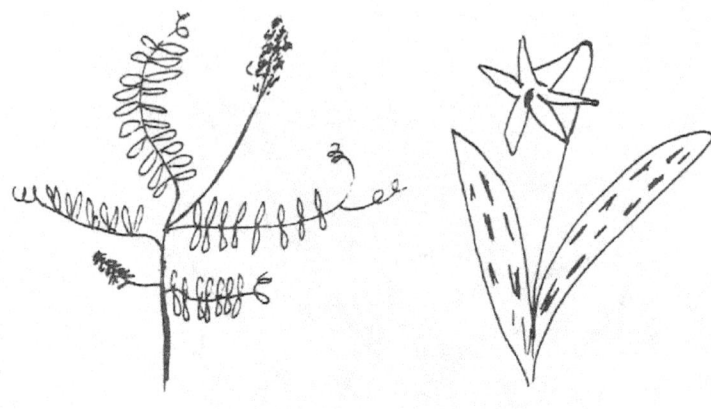

Fig. 119   Vetch   Fig. 120   Trout Lily

YELLOW NUTSEDGE (CHUFA)   *Cyperus esculentus*   **Figure 118**

The yellow nutsedge is found throughout the United States and southern Canada. It reproduces by seeds and weak thread-like stolons terminated by hard nut tubers. The leaves are in groups of three grasslike sheaths found along the stem. Spike flower heads develop into a fan shaped array of wide angled flowers.

Once chufa takes root it becomes a serious weed if it is not welcome. The small nutlike tubers on the roots are edible, raw or cooked. Unless you find a crop in loose sandy soils the nuts are likely to be hard and almost impossible to crush with the teeth unless cooked. Cook by baking or roasting or boiling. Roasted chufa nuts may be ground into flour and made into a fine coffee.

VI
NOTES ON FUNGI AND LICHENS

Ganoderma lucidiumaa do not eat this fungus

PUFFBALLS *Lycoperdon and Calvatia species*

All puffballs are edible and should only be collected when young and firm. Any dark colored puffball should not be eaten. Young puffballs can be cooked directly. The giant puffball, *Calvatia gigantea*, should be peeled before frying or cooking. Puffballs are delicious sliced and fried or cut into bits and mixed with scrambled eggs. Be sure you have a puffball and not a mushroom in the button stage.

MUSHROOMS   Figure 121   Figure 122

Although there are more edible mushrooms than poisonous mushrooms it is best to keep away from them entirely unless you are personally acquainted with someone who will show them to you and eat them with you. Eating them on the basis of handbook descriptions are at best hazardous. Do not believe folk ways for finding out if the mushrooms are edible or not. One of these popular superstitions concerning mushrooms is that if they are boiled with a silver coin and the coin turns black the mushrooms are poisonous. Don't try any such foolishness, buy your mushrooms commercially.

There are two great edible species that once recognized are easy to recognize again. These are the meadow mushroom *Agaricus arvensis* and *Agaricus campestris* which is found in pastures and cow meadows in and around cow manure, and the early

Fig. 121   Early Inky Mushroom   Fig. 122   Edible Morel

inky mushroom found around dead or decayed stumps and are called by the collectors as "stumpies." Again I must emphasize, don't eat them without the approval and guidance of someone who does not rely upon superstition for his source of information. These species of mushrooms are edible   Do not attempt to eat them unless you are sure of yourself.

Agaricus arvensis	field mushroom
Agaricus campestris	meadow mushroom
Armillaria mellea	honey mushroom
Cantharellus cibarius	chanterelle
Clavaria pulchra	yellow club
Clavaria umbonatus	grayling
Collybia radicata	root mushroom
Collybia velutipes	velvet collybia
Coprinus atramentarius	ink cap
Coprinus comatus	shaggy mane
Coprinus micaceus (Fig. 121	early inky mushroom
Fistulina hepatica	beafsteak mushroom
Hydnum caputursi	bears head
Hydnum corralloides	coral fungus
Hypholoma perplexum	red hypholoma
Lactarius deliciosus	milky mushroom*
Lepiota procera	parasol mushroom
Marasmius oreades	fairy ring
Morchella esculenta (Fig. 122	morel mushroom
Pleurotus ostreatus	oyster mushroom
Pleurotus ulmarius	elm mushroom
Pluteus cervinus	pluteus
Polyporus sulphureus	sulphur mushroom
Russula virescens	green russula
Steccherinum	see Hydnum above
Strobilomyces strobilaceus	pine cone mushroom

Some general rules for beginners on what to avoid when gathering mushrooms are (1) avoid any species you do not know to be edible (2) avoid any mushrooms beginning to show age (3)

*Many milky mushrooms are poisonous and even though this specimen is edible one should be cautious of any which oozes a milky juice.

Figure 123: Bear's Head fungus, *Hydnum caputursi*

Figure 124 : Shaggy Mane mushroom, *Coprinus comatus*

avoid all mushrooms in the button stage (4) avoid all mushrooms with a scaly bulb at the base of the stem (5) avoid all mushrooms with small pores under the cap (6) avoid woodland mushrooms with a bright red cap and white gills below (7) avoid yellow orange mushrooms in late summer growing at the base of stumps, and (8) avoid any mushroom with white milky juice.

LICHENS

ICELAND MOSS   *Cetraria islandica*

This is a tufted lichen, it appears as olive drab mats with red splotches. Funnel shaped tufts rise and divide at their summits from the mats. It is a ground plant which is highly nutritious. If it appears to be bitter then a second boiling is in order.

Figure 125

ROCK TRIPE   *Umbilicaria pustulata*   Figure 127

This is a lichen which grows on boulders and jutting rocks usually in highland regions. It appears as rubbery plates, gray to greenish in color above and tan below. The upper surface on some species appears to have bubbles or blisters on it. These can be boiled slowly for about an hour and served as soup. For real zest throw in a few wild onion bulbs.

Fig. 125   Rock Tripe

Figure 126

Deadly Amanita

THE DEADLY AMANITA
Figure 126

One of the deadliest plants in nature is the Amanita mushroom, also known as the destroying angel mushroom and death angel mushroom. Its ghostly white form emerges in the woods, defying animals to eat it. When humans eat it, there is no antidote, and a painful death follows.

As young Amanitas emerge they are covered with a baglike veil or volva. This tissue is loose and crumbly and gives way as the stem elongates and grows which forces the emerging cap through the veil. Puffballs are edible and delicious. However, a death angel mushroom in its button stage looks like a puffball. Therefore, when picking puffballs avoid the very small ones. Puffballs almost always grow in open fields or pasture grounds while Amanitas are nearly always in woodlands.

Deadly Amanita mushrooms grow in woods. They are tall and conspicuous. The death angel is white but other Amanitas may be yellowish, orangish, brownish, olive, and blackish. The surface of the cap may have traces of the veil on it in the form of warts or patches. These can be picked off.

Gills on the death angel are white but some may be tinged with red or yellow. The stems are quite long and have a bulb at the base. There is a ring around the stem. This ring and bulb at the base are the best identifications marks of Amanita.

The active poison in the death angel may persist in dried mushrooms up to ten years. Boiling does not get rid of the toxin. Once eaten, the victim begins to vomit after about six hours and has violent stomach pains. This is followed by thirst and diarrhea. The pains are so severe that the face becomes distorted and jaundice may appear. A coma develops and the patient dies. Death is due to extreme fatty degeneration of the liver. Some people have eaten small amounts of the death angel mushroom and lived. Many people have died from eating just a small fragment of the cap.

Alcohol should never by given to a person who has eaten a poison mushroom since this acts to quickly spread the poison to all parts of the body. This disease is complicated by the fact that the liver sends the poison to the kidneys which rejects it and sends it back to the liver. This ping-pong game between the organs with the poison prevents any effective treatment.

Fortunately there are not many poison mushrooms compared to the number which can be eaten. However, poison mushrooms are so deadly that any mushroom picker should invest a little time in learning their differences.

Figure 127: Rock tripe, *Umbilicaria pustulata*

VII
USEFUL HERBS
AND SOME OPINIONS

Figure 128: Tansy, *Tanacetum vulgare*

HERBAL MEDICINE GAINS POPULARITY

There is renewed interest in medicinal herbs in our country. Previously herb usage was confined to hill country people, native Americans and isolated groups such as the Amish. But with the side effects of modern drugs, the expense of physicians, and general distrust in institutions, there is a movement back to the old ways when herbs were a natural part of healing.

Herbaceous plants are distinguished from woody plants. A herb is generally considered a plant whose stem is soft and green and shows little growth of wood. Most herbaceous plants die after one season of growth. For centuries herbs have been used as medicines, spices, and for mystical purposes.

Herbals were books used in the fifteenth and sixteenth centuries. These books contained descriptions and illustrations of plants with those properties that made them useful in medicine and cooking. A few Herbals were directed at making spells and potions. Most of them were based on unfounded assumptions. But the illustrations were excellent and many of them can be purchased today in reprints of rare books.

The main theory behind herb medicine was the idea that parts of plants resemble parts of human beings. For instance, the walnut resembled the brain and hence walnuts were considered good for headaches and other brain disorders. Heart shaped leaves were thought to relieve heart disease. Flowers with long stems were considered good for throat ailments. Plants with reddish sap, such as bloodroot, were used to treat blood disorders. Hundreds of plants were considered able to remove warts. Today ginseng is still regarded as a health-giving plant although no scientific evidence exists to confirm this.

One of the biggest booms in small business is the herbal tea industry which has netted over a hundred million dollars every year since 1970. But most people can gather their own herbs and make their own tea. Some of the most commonly used plants for natural teas are the mints, chamomile, rose hips, sour grass, strawberry, and sumac berries (which are not in the herb class).

Herb teas are made by simply pouring hot water over the fresh or dried parts of the plants, mainly leaves and twigs. It is not a good idea to use wilted plants since these will usually build up toxins which are expelled by drying and which do not exist in fresh leaves and stems.

THE TEA SHOP

Several years ago I opened a tea shop: I was interested in the subject and there was a vacant shop available. My tea business lasted about two years and afforded me a chance to sample exotic teas and gather information on this aspect of plants.

One woman who was a regular customer complained that chamomile tea made her break out in a rash. This seemed strange to me since the teas that I sold were only those tested over many years and even centuries. If I had a strange tea I used it myself and didn't sell it.

My daughter Becky had been getting allergy shots about this time and she suggested that the woman was allergic to chamomile or plants related to it. As it turned out chamomile belonged to the same family of plants as daisy, asters, and ragweed. Ordinarily a person sensitive to ragweed would not be affected, but her sensitivity was extreme, even to daisies. The woman underwent the usual sensitivity tests and was prescribed medication which she will have to take the rest of her life.

I had written a book on edible wild plants and included a chapter on poisonous plants similar to the one in this book. Poisonous plants are not necessarily lethal, but they do cause hallucinations and numbing. A student at the local college visited me at the end of one summer. He wanted to know more about herbs. I discussed these with him thinking that he was doing a biology project.

It turned out the student was drying, cooking, stewing, baking, and eating and smoking the poisonous herbs. He had tried such deadly poisonous plant parts as the leaves of nightshade and jimson weed, the seeds of jimson weed, poison ivy, and pokeweed. He said he was in a stupor for about a week from smoking certain dried mushrooms and that he was giving it all up. I got the feeling that he was talking to me to get more information for further experimentation. I stopped giving him my ideas on it and tried to get a list of plants he used and his reactions to them. He promised to give me the list but the next I knew he had gone back to New Jersey.

AMISH FRIENDS

Amish people have a reputation for being close to nature and using folk medicine. I was fortunate enough to work with a group of four Amish men and one woman on a construction project over a summer. I learned a lot about Amish culture and the different herbs they used. They liked teas made from various kinds of mint which they then perked up with lemon. This was a strong brew which was too much for me and I stuck to my teas although I drank theirs occasionally.

The oldest man, known as "Pappy" said he had originally lived in Ohio.

When Amish move, they take roots from their old garden with them. Pappy had brought his mint with him and made a weakened mixture for me. It was good and he agreed to give me some roots from his mint patch.

One day Mose, a fellow worker, got ill and Pappy went out into the brush and came back with bunches of plants. He set them down, studied them for a while, then asked Mose to describe his ailment. Pappy diagnosed his complaint as stomach trouble and brewed up a pot of boneset tea which he insisted Mose drink. Mose looked to me hoping I would come to his rescue, but the Amish elders have the final word and he drank the tea with a horrible expression. The next day Mose was feeling fine and everyone agreed it must have been Pappy's tea.

When another member of the crew got a cut Pappy put some yarrow leaves over it and wrapped it. He wanted the man to let his dog lick it first but the man was not about to do that. The cut did heal quickly.

Perhaps the Amish I met on the construction crew were not typical of their group but they seemed to speak for the entire community. Although they had a lot of success with their medicinal plants, I still believe modern drugs are better for cases of severe illness.

Amish put a lot of faith in various leaves placed in shoes to relieve colds and other respiratory problems. Chest remedies were a common practice with Pappy. That summer Mose's four children came down with whooping cough (Most Amish do not immunize their children). Mose had some herbal extract delivered to him from another Amish community; this, he said, would break up the cough. Each child's illness lasted about six weeks which is roughly normal for the disease.

INDIAN DOCTORS

There is something in me which wants to believe in herbal practitioners. Foremost among these are the Indian doctors who live in fact as well as legend. Most of these "medicine men" practiced what can best be described as "faith healing." I have great faith in "faith" healing and the power of positive thinking. However, we must acknowledge that there are some ailments that only modern medicine can cure.

Probably the most famous Indian doctor of the east was Joe Pye after whom the plant was named. Old Joe would lace teas made from members of the boneset family with rum or other strong spirits and prescribe this by the whiskey-glass full. It is claimed that he worked many cures. Every once in a while I make a mint tea and lace it with whiskey and take the Joe Pye cure.

My mother had a limp when she walked. My oldest sister told me that this affliction had occurred during the birth of my next oldest brother.

One day an Indian doctor arrived at our house in southwestern Pennsylvania having been sent to us from the mountains somewhere near Somerset, Pennsylvania. He promised mother relief and cure for her bad leg. I was about five years old at the time and very impressed with his demeanor.

The Indian disappeared into the hills around home for a day and reappeared the next day with an assortment of herbs. He gave mother a collection of large soft leaves to put in her shoe. Other leaves and stems were made into several concoctions which were preserved in bottles, about a dozen in all. For this service he charged my mother ten dollars, which she gladly paid. My father's income as a coal miner at that time was twelve dollars a week.

My mother's limp never went away but there was useful knowledge gained from the experience. Sometimes the knowledge gained from things that don't work is just as important as knowledge gained from things which do work. My mother learned not to expect miracles and I not yet in school learned something about life and plants.

As I roamed the hillsides about home I found most of the plants the Indian doctor had used. As I grew older I learned their names.

He had used mullein leaves for the shoe inserts and the liquid concoctions were made from ground ivy, sassafras leaves and stems, curly dock root, and healall.

This experience did not make me skeptical but it did teach me to approach some aspects of life with caution. It was the beginning of an education which would convince me that all life was dependent upon each other for existence and that there is a dependent relationship between plants and animals which should not be ignored.

MYSTICAL EXPERIENCES

Many years ago I was clearing a roadway through my brush and trees when I cut down a rather large tree. Curious about its age, I counted the tree rings. There were 36 rings; add one year for seedling, thus the tree was thirty-seven years old — the same age I was at the time.

Then it hit me: the realization that I had killed a living thing. It took some time before I could bring myself to continue clearing brush and cutting trees; there was a strong feeling of actual communication with trees, the oldest living things on earth. I have never gotten over the fact that all animals must consume living or once living tissue to remain alive be it plant or animal.

Bonnie and I visited Taiwan a few years after this experience. There on the slopes of Bamboo Mountain were large trees enclosed with fences. The fences were built by Buddhists who venerated these giant cedars; the trees were actually shrines where people came to worship.

Also on Taiwan we visited the Bunam people, an aboriginal tribe living in an area of mountains and lakes. These extremely religious people have almost 200 holy days a year.

Among their beliefs is the idea of tree species having a spirit which watches over that particular species. When they cut down a tree they recite a poem prayer to the appropriate tree spirit. The prayer explains the reasons for cutting down the tree and why it is needed.

Today I still cut down trees and clear brush. But every now and then, especially when I destroy a tree with perfect symmetry, beautiful leaves, delicate buds and fruits, I begin to wonder once more what life is all about and I find myself unconsciously apologizing to the tree spirit.

Endangered Species

Some plants are just as endangered as animals. What difference does it make if a plant goes out of existence? Well, by saving endangered plant species we save their genetic pool for future generations. As gene splicing becomes more common new varieties of plants will be crossed.

About 90 percent of all medicines used today come from plants or are chemical reproductions of plant products. Medicinal break-throughs are occuring every year by plant research. A new extract of the periwinkle plant has recently been successful in combating leukemia. Native Americans and others living close to nature have always used plants to combat illness. For instance, they chewed on willow bark to relieve pain. It turned out that willow bark has the same chemical properties as aspirin.

What the Indians and other ancients couldn't do was to concentrate the healing chemicals of plants. With modern chemistry this can be done and about one-fourth of all prescriptions handed over the counter today are pure plant extracts. Most others are reproductions of chemical compounds first discovered in plants.

The moral here is that we should support the concept of protecting endangered plant species, since some day the plant may be called upon to protect us.

Herb Festival

Although there are only four seasons in Japan rural people celebrate them with five festivals. The first of these in the new year is the Festival of The Young Herbs, which is also known as the Festival of The Seven Grasses.

The festival dates back to the feudal days of the shogun. Even though most of the significance of the festival has disappeared many urban Japanese still celebrate the season by going out into rural areas to acquire the herbs and grasses.

The wild plants are gathered, boiled slightly, and mixed with a rice gruel. Most of the urban Japanese, who are returning to the old values, are trying to learn the seven plants; but, with difficulty in identification they settle for less than seven, or substitute a known edible plant native to their own area.

The original seven plants are watercress, cottonweed, shepherd's purse, chickweed, nipplewort, wild turnip leaves, and wild radish leaves. Common substitutions for these plants are parsley, spinach, carrot leaves, cabbage, dandelion, various tree buds, and burdock.

The ancients pounded the plants on a wood block and mixed them with well water. During the ritual there were various words to be chanted or sung. One of the songs goes something like this:

> Let us gather
> The seven herbs of spring
> Before the Chinese birds come
> To eat them with the birds of Japan.

The festival is held in the middle of the month of January or at the beginning of the calendar year. However, by interpreting the meaning of the festival to be during the first week of the lunar year the Japanese are assured a larger variety of spring shoots for the ceremony.

You can make your own Japanese Festival by gathering the edible green shoots of spring. Mix them with rice gruel to which well water has been added.

SPRING TONICS

The generation before mine grew up with "spring tonics." As winter snow melted people began to drink some sort of wild tea or eat certain plants to restore the body and thin the blood. They ate dandelions, chickweed, yellow rocket, skunk cabbage, and water cress. They drank teas and juices made from sassafras, mint, chickweed, strawberry leaves, and violet leaves. Apparently these worked because people said they felt better.

Over the winter some people did develop usually mild (but sometime severe) cases of scurvy due to the lack of Vitamin C in their diets. Transportation systems were not then what they are today. Today we can purchase oranges and other fruits in any season thanks to modern trucking and aircraft. But when I was a lad we were fortunate to get an orange in our Christmas stocking. In those days it was difficult to transport fresh fruits and vegetables from warmer regions to colder ones. Thus, there was a lack of Vitamin C and to some extent Vitamin A in the diet; so the wild spring tonics did work to restore health and vitality.

Euell Gibbons, who probably gave more talks and wrote more about edible and useful wild plants than anyone else, was often asked about the nutritional value of wild plants. The subject intrigued him and he personally paid for a study to examine a variety of wild plants for their nutritional values. It was discovered that many wild plant were far superior to domesticated plants in both nutrition and food value.

Gibbon s'study found the following to be very high in Vitamins C and A: curly dock, winter cress, green amaranth, nettles, violet leaves, lambs quarters, pokeweed shoots, high bush cranberry fruits, watercress, and spearmint. Catnip leaves, persimmons, ground ivy, violet blossoms, and wild strawberry leaves were all high in Vitamin C but just average in Vitamin A content. Dandelion green, lambs quarters, blackberries, ground cherries, red haws, persimmons, black and red raspberries, and gooseberries were higher in calories than domestic plants. Gibbons found that red haws had more calories (food energy) than any of the common domestic fruits including apples, oranges, and peaches.

NATIVE AMERICAN USE OF HERBS

Literature is beginnning to accumulate about the Native American's use of wild plants for food and medicine. Many believe these native cures are better than modern medicine. Some of the native cures were effective but it must be remembered that Native Americans had no knowledge of the microbiologic or viral origin of diseases. Their remedies were most effective in the treatment of nutritional diseases. They also had some success treating mental and nervous disorders indicating that some of these disorders may be chemical or nutritional in nature.

So we can say Native Americans used wild herbs to treat disorders and symptoms rather than diseases; disorders like diarrhea, fever, non-congenital eye and ear problems, headaches, nausea, and general stomach and digestive problems. You cannot treat epidemics, broken bones, congenital problems, or cellular disorders effectively with herbs. However, the concentrated extracts of some herbs may be effective in treating such problems, especially where narcotics are needed.

According to interviews with Native Americans and eye witness accounts of their behavior they used the following to treat common disorders:

Circulatory disorders - oak, dogbane, calamus, wild onion, cowslip, burdock, goldenrod

Convulsions - dogbane, goldenrod, wild rose, hickory leaves

Cuts and wounds - chokecherry leaves, pulverized curly dock root, white pine bark,hemlock bark, puffball spores, yarrow

Diarrhea - mullein, nettles, raspberry roots, mint tea, chokecherry fruit, thistle roots, rose roots, yarrow, a mash of green herbs and charcoal was very effective

Ear disorders - drops of mullein flower oil, yarrow, elderberry juice, compresses of hot wild onion, Solomon Seal root

Eyes - eyewashes of wintergreen, blackberry roots, yarrow leaves, compresses of mashed Solomon Seal root

Fever - catnip, goldenrod

Indigestion and stomach pains - wild ginger, arrowhead, willow, black birch, smartweed, nettle, black haw, bloodroot

Rheumatism - juniper, yew, wild grapes, plantain, spruce needles

Sore mouth and throat - calamus, chokecherry, wild ginger, slippery elm, sumac gargle, white waterlily, tansy

Spitting up blood - goldenrod, chokecherry, oak

Urinary problems - nettle, goldenrod, snowberry, cowslip

PIONEER FOLK CURES

In the early days of America's pioneers doctors were scarce and people had to rely on folk remedies to cure their illnesses. Often these cures were a blend of truth, luck, and superstition; prayer was often relied upon as part of the cure.

The human body is a miraculous organism which is designed to heal itself and generally it will do this over a period of time whether or not the illness is treated. Modern medicines merely aid in reducing the discomfort of most ailments. Older folk remedies tended to do the same thing although folk wisdom held that "to be effective, medicine has to taste bad and the external applications have to be uncomfortable."

Today, there is a swing back toward folk medicine and many books on the subject are finding their way into modern homes. Most of the early folk medicine remedies relied upon herbs, sometimes including various animal extracts. Since this was all these pioneers had to work with this is what they used.

Coughs and respiratory afflictions were treated with an extract of snakeroot which is poisonous. The snakeroot extracts were diluted or adulterated to keep body responses to the poison to a minimum. Honey was also used often to ease the throat. A most pleasant cure was a hot blanket wrap accompanied by soaking feet in hot water while taking a shot of whiskey. Various poultices were also applied, including the infamous mustard plaster.

Rheumatism was treated with an extract of bloodroot or various bark oils as well as grease from mammals, birds, and snakes. These extracts and oils were rubbed on the afflicted area.

Dysentery and diarrhea were treated with teas made from just about every wild plant available. One of the more popular plants was the mayapple or mandrake root which is also quite poisonous.

Blood letting was popular in pioneer days but seems to have disappeared in modern times. Teas were also heated to boiling and applied as compresses to the stomach to alleviate the pain associated with dysentery.

Eye inflammations were treated with goldenseal and jimson weed. Roots of these plants were boiled and after the liquid cooled it was applied to the inflamed eye.

Burns were helped with poultices made of potato mash, turnips, various barks, and ground grains. Wrapping the wound with cabbage leaves seemed to have been a favorite treatment of burns. Wood ashes were also sprinkled on the wound, often leaving scars when healed.

Insect and snake bites were treated with concoctions designed to draw out the poisons. These were usually derivatives made from barks of nut trees or direct applications of plants such as fern and plantain.

Itching was cured by the juice of jewel weed or other watery plants. Pioneers used jewel weed to cure athlete's foot. It was found that jewel weed contains a fungicide.

Severe skin problems were also given a sulfur and lard treatment. Poison ivy rashes were avoided by a quick application of the juice of jewel weed immediately after contact. The poison ivy plant was also used as preventative medicine, for such ailments as thin blood, boils, and the ague.

Certain plants and animals seem to be favorites of today's folk healers - mayapple, jewel weed, jimson weed, goldenseal, various mushrooms, slippery elm, walnut, white oak, mullein, bloodroot, poison ivy, snakeroot, anise, and practically anything called an herb. The favorite animal by far is the rattlesnake probably because it symbolizes mystery and strength. Animals of lesser potency include the black bear, raccoon, opossum, toad, weasel, mink, salamander, and crow. Usually some portion of the animal such as the bear gall bladder, raccoon claws, toad hides, weasel urine is used and the rest of the animal is discarded.

Credibility is suspect when one plant contains the cures for a variety of unrelated ailments. For example, dogwood bark, fruit, and flowers are used to treat muscle aches, fevers, liver problems, and malaria. Spicebush tea and powdered bark is used to treat lung ailments, chills and fever, as well as intestinal worms.

Some folk treatments rely too heavily on magic and superstition. For instance, there are two popular methods for getting rid of warts. You rub the warts with peach leaves and bury the leaves in the backyard. As the leaves rot away so do the warts. In the other tried and true method you get water from the stump of a cut off tree and rub this on the warts as you walk around the tree three times saying "warts be gone."

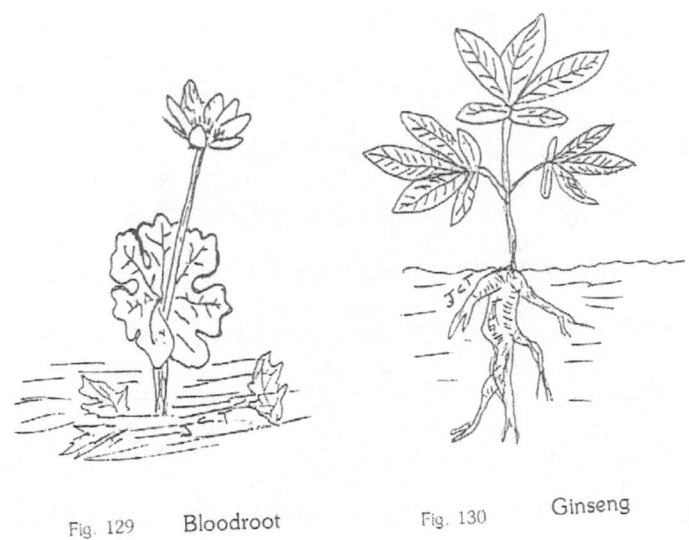

Fig. 129   Bloodroot   Fig. 130   Ginseng

BLOODROOT   *Sanguinaria canadensis*   **Figure 129**

Bloodroot grows to eight inches under ideal conditions. Look for white flowers with golden centers, each on a single stem. Its stem and root is filled with red sap fluid.

Although bloodroot has been used for centuries in folk medicine, its curative powers seem to be no more potent than any other plant. It was used effectively as a dye for Indian baskets and ornaments as well as a paint for the face which also served to ward off insects.

The bloodroot root is irritating to the stomach when dried and ingested. It creates nausea and vomiting when taken internally.

GINSENG   *Panax quinquefolius*   **Figure 130**

Ginseng has three leaf stems, each divided into 5 toothed leaflets. In spring it bears white flowers in a cluster which give rise to red berries in the fall. Wonderful medicinal powers have been ascribed to ginseng roots. Despite the fact that modern medicine has not been able to effectively document ginseng's medicinal powers there is a brisk trade of the roots in America and an enormous trade in Asia.

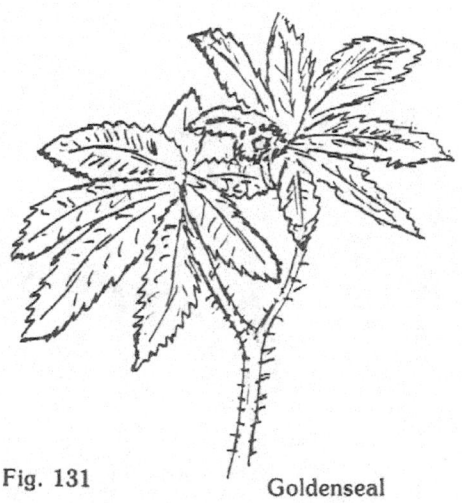

Fig. 131   Goldenseal

GOLDENSEAL   *Hydrastis canadensis*   **Figure 131**
   The goldenseal may grow to 18 inches. Its yellowish flower becomes a small bunch of red berries in the fall. It has hairy leaves. The goldenseal is rare and should not be picked. It was once abundant but its use as a medicinal herb has placed it on the endangered list. The thick yellow root was used as well as the leaves and stem. Goldenseal is used to treat sore throat, sore mouth and gums, skin infections, genital irritations, stomach ulcers, and intestinal bleeding. It makes a bitter tea.

JUNIPER   *Juniperus virginiana*
The eastern red cedar or juniper berries are edible in small quantities. It is the major flavoring in gin. The tree grows in open woods. It is an evergreen with two types of twigs, often on the same tree. Young twigs are sharply pointed while older twigs which bear the fruit are often scaly. The fruit is a bluish berry covered with a whitish powder and has a resinous quality about it.

Fig. 132

HEALALL *Prunella vulgaris* A. habit of growth B. flower C. calyx
D. seeds

HEALALL   *Prunella vulgaris*   **Figure 132**
  Healall, also known as prunella, has two-lipped tubular purplish flowers.
Since its flowers have a yawning appearance, ancient peoples believed it
to be an effective throat medicine. It has been used to clean fresh wounds
without any ill effects. It does not live up to its name or its undeserved reputation as a healing plant. It was also used by Native Americans to treat
dysentery in infants.

MUGWORT *Artemisia vulgaris* A. habit of growth B. enlarged leaves C. panicle of flowers D. flower head E. flowers F. achenes

Fig. 133

Fig. 134

COMMON MULLEIN *Verbascum thapsus*   A. habit B. flower C. capsules D. seeds

Fig. 135·

PRICKLY LETTUCE   *Lactuca serriola*   A. habit of growth B. flower
heads C. seeds

MUGWORT   *Artemisia vulgaris*   Figure 133

Mugwort is an aromatic perennial herb. Its green leaves are white and wooly beneath. Mugwort, also known as wormwood, leaves may be used for flavoring drinks or they may be dried for use as an aromatic culinary herb.

Mugwort has been used extensively in Indian and folk medicine. A mugwort poultice was used on wounds. They put mugwort leaves in their nostrils to cure a headache. Although there may be curative powers in mugwort most of the early uses (to induce labor, to protect travelers) have little basis in reality.

MULLEIN   *Verbascum thapsus*   Figure 134

Mullein is a biennial herb reproducing by seeds. Its stout stem sometimes reaches nine feet high. It's leaves and stem are covered with wooly hairs.

Mullein looks like a plant that should have many uses. It is used in many ways but none of these amount to much. A tea of the dried leaves is said to relieve coughs and bronchial complaints. Early settlers used it to control constipation and ease the pain of hemorrhoids. The ancients made a shampoo of the flowers which tinted the hair yellow.

PRICKLY LETTUCE   *Lactuca scariola*   Figure 135

This annual wild lettuce has milky juice and a large taproot. Stems are pale green with lower portions prickly. Leaves are bluish green with prickly toothed edges. Flowers are pale yellow with ray flowers appearing blue when dried.

Pick only the small leaves when they first emerge and use them raw in salads. If cooked, boil them only about two minutes before serving. Cover with regular salad dressing.

All species of wild lettuce are edible. Native Americans used the wild lettuce as a sedative, eating the gum formed by hardening of the milky juice. Eating a large amount of the young leaves is said to put one in a mood of tranquility.

YARROW   *Achillea millefolium*   Figure 136

This perennial herb reproduces by seeds and underground roots. The stem is simple with some forking at the top leading to white disk flowers. Finely segmented leaves emerge from the stems.

Yarrow is reputed to have been used by Native Americans to cure many ills once the plant was brought from Europe. Yarrow will stop the flow of blood in small wounds and it will accelerate healing. A shampoo of the mashed weed is reputed to prevent baldness. To make a drink for colds and fevers pour hot water over dried yarrow leaves. Drink only a small glass at a time to see how you react to it. Sweeten it with honey if you decide it's helping you.

Figure 136

COMMON YARROW *Achillea millefolium* A. plant B. leaves and stem C. flower head D. female and male flowers E. seeds

SLIPPERY ELM
(Ulmus fulva)

Fig. 137

SLIPPERY ELM   *Ulmus fulva*   Figure 137

Elm leaves are broadly elliptical with parallel veins and toothed edges. The seeds are surrounded by thin hairy collars notched at the tip. Despite the Dutch Elm Disease the slippery elm can still be found in abundance in our woods. The inner bark of the tree can be dried, pulverized, and ground into flour. The inner bark can be chewed upon raw just for curiosity but one would hardly dine on it in that condition.

Pulverized elm bark is a widely used medicine in rural areas. It can sometimes be purchased in pharmacies. It has been used effectively as an expectorant, diuretic, and laxative. When mixed with water the powdered elm bark makes a soothing dressing for irritated skin. It should be valued for its nutrition.

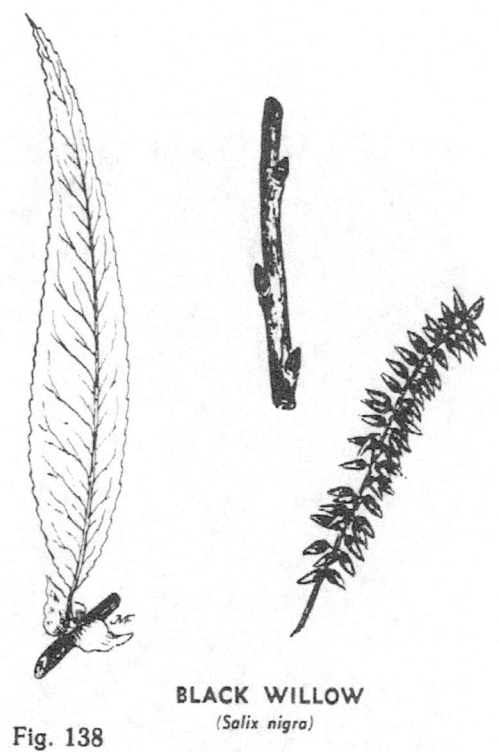

BLACK WILLOW
(Salix nigra)

Fig. 138

WILLOW   *Salix species*   Figure 138

Willows have lance shaped leaves and a single cap scale on the bud. The male and female flower clusters are separate. Willows are found most often around moist areas. They become a nuisance in low lying areas making travel difficult.

Willow bark contains a pain reliever and chewing on the bark has long been a treatment for toothache and muscular pains. However, too much bark will upset one's stomach.

Poultices of willow leaves, roots, and stems have been used effectively to relieve pain in the afflicted areas since medicines can be absorbed through the skin.

Washing in a willow solution will aid in treating dandruff. Native Americans used a strong solution of the leaves to treat diarrhea. The Willow stems were also reduced to charcoal and taken for the same ailment.

John Tomikel

Photo taken at a wild foods gathering in summer 1984
when Dr. Tomikel was 56 years old.

RECOMMENDED
FOR FURTHER REFERENCE

Berglund, B. and C.E. Bolsby, 1971, *The Edible Wild*, Charles Scribner's Sons

Brockman, C. Frank, 1968, *Trees of North America*, Golden Field Guide: Illustrated by Rebecca Merrilees

Coon, V., 1957, *Using wayside plants*, Hearthside Press Inc.

Crockett, Lawrence J., 1977, *Wildly Successful Plants*, Collier Books: Illustrated by Joanne Bradley (Among the best plant illustrations I have seen)

Densmore, Frances, 1926, *How Indians Use Wild Plants for Food, Medicine, and Crafts*, Dover Reprint

Gibbons, E., 1962, *Stalking the wild asparagus*, David McKay Co.

Gibbons, Euell, 1964, *Stalking the Blue Eyed Scallop*, David McKay Co.

Gibbons, Euell, 1966, *Stalking The Healthful Herbs*, David McKay Co.

Gillespie, W., 1959, *Edible Wild Plants of West Virginia*, Scholars Library

Hedrick, U.P., 1972, *Sturtevant's Edible Plants of the World*, Dover Publications

Hitchcock, Susan Tyler, 1980, *Gather Ye Wild Things*, Harper and Row: Illustrated by G.B. McIntosh

Keeler, H., 1969, *Our Northern Shrubs*, Dover Publications

Krieger, Louis C.C., 1936, *The Mushroom Handbook*, Dover Reprint, Illustrated by the author

Medsger, O., 1966, *Edible Wild Plants*, Macmillan Company

North American Wildlife, Reader's Digest Field Guide (One of the best of its kind)

Petrides, George A., 1958, *A Field Guide To Trees and Schrubs*, Second Edition Houghton Mifflin

Rollins, R. and M. Fernold and A. Kinsey, 1958, *Edible Wild Plants*, Harper

Saunders, Charles Francis, 1920, *Edible and Useful Wild Plants Of The United States and Canada*, Dover Reprint: Some illustrations by Lucy Hamilton Aring

Scully, Virginia, 1975, *A Treasure of American Indian Foods*, Bonanza Books

Tomikel, J., 1973, *Edible Wild Plants of Pennsylvania and New York*, Allegheny Press

Tomikel, J., 1976, *Edible Wild Plants of Eastern United States and Canada*, Allegheny Press

Tomikel, J., 1978, *Wild Foods Cookery*, Allegheny Press

U.S. Dept. of Agriculture, 1971, *Common Weeds of the United States*, Dover Publications

Wherry, E., 1948, *Wild Flower Guide*, Doubleday

INDEX

Credits

The full page drawings of plants are by Regina O. Hughes of the U.S. Department of Agriculture.

The half page drawings of tree parts are by J. M. Francis of the Department of Agriculture, State of Pennsylvania

The cover sketch is from an old woodcut.

All photographs and sketches are by John Tomikel except those on pages 6,11,12,18,131 which are from Wikipedia.

Caution

Some road and railroads spray their right-of-ways with defoliants to keep down weeds.

Avoid any areas that have a patch of dried leaves on each side of the road or railroad.

Keep in mind that a weed is a good plant that happens to be in our way at the time.

www.ingramcontent.com/pod-product-compliance
Lightning Source LLC
Chambersburg PA
CBHW060511290526

45791CB00001B/361